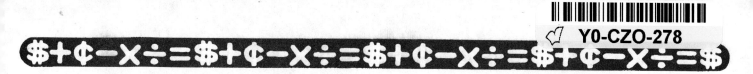
Instructional Fair's *Math Topics — Grade 6* is just one of a series of Basic Skills books that can be used by parents, teachers or tutors to help students master essential skills taught in the sixth grade.

This book has been designed both to instruct students and to provide them with practice in mathematical concepts taught at the sixth grade level. Each skill/concept is presented on two pages. The first page includes step-by-step instructions and guided practice. This does not take away the need for instruction of the skill, but rather reviews the skill taught, enabling the student to work independently with examples to follow. The guided practice serves to reinforce the skill/concept before students go on to the second page. The second page features a fun type of activity and allows for independent practice. These activity pages have many formats including crossword puzzles, mazes and decoding messages. They are designed to let students have fun as they practice new mathematical skills.

Ideally, the skills/concepts presented in this book will be taught in the classroom or at home using manipulatives. Students will be better able to grasp the material with the use of concrete objects, especially if they have problems with a particular skill.

Besides teachers, tutors and parents will also find this book useful. The instructional page can be done along with the student, and the fun practice page will show that not all math homework has to be dry and boring. Some of it can actually be enjoyable!

This book covers 21 sixth grade mathematical concepts. The answers to the activities can be found on pages 44-48. Other books with this same format for sixth grade that you might wish to consider include *Decimals and Percents* and *Fractions*.

Geometric Figures

Example	Description	Symbol	Read
Point • A	A point is an end of a line segment (an exact location in space).	A	point A
Line E D	A line is a collection of points in a straight path that extends in two directions without end.	$\overleftrightarrow{DE}$	line DE
Line Segment R ——— S	A line segment is part of a line with two endpoints.	$\overline{RS}$	segment RS
Ray B ——→ C	A ray is part of a line having only one endpoint.	$\overrightarrow{BC}$	ray BC
Angle C D ——→ E	An angle is two rays having a common endpoint.	$\angle CDE$	angle CDE
Plane T S U	A plane is an endless flat surface.	plane STU	plane STU

Use the figure to name each.

1. 1 ray

2. a plane

3. 3 points

4. 2 lines

5. 3 angles

6. 3 line segments

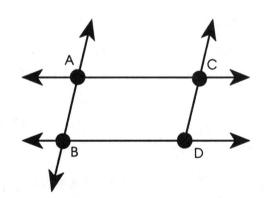

2

Gee Ahm Confused!

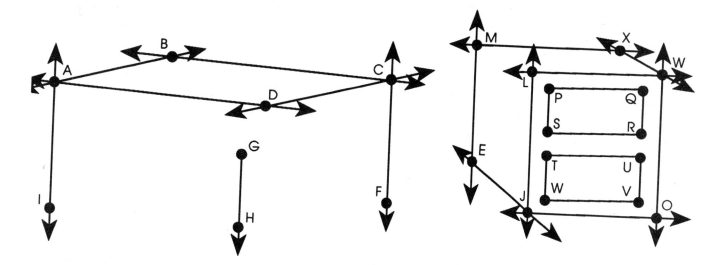

Use the figure to name each.

1. 6 line segments
2. 2 planes
3. 5 rays

4. 7 points
5. 6 lines
6. 5 angles

Draw and label each figure.

1. ray CD
2. point X
3. segment AB

4. plane WXY
5. angle DFG
6. line MN

Classifying Angles

| **Angle** | two rays (sides) having a common vertex |

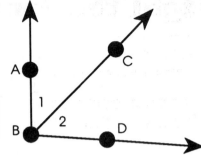

| **Example 1** |

y = vertex

2 rays = $\overrightarrow{YX}$, $\overrightarrow{YZ}$

3 ways to name the angle

∠1

∠Y

∠XYZ (The vertex is always the middle letter.)

| **Example 2** |

3 angles are represented:

∠1 = ∠ABC = ∠CBA

∠2 = ∠CBD = ∠DBC

∠ABD = ∠DBA

Classifying Angles

Right	**Acute**	**Obtuse**	**Straight**
measures exactly 90°	measures less than 90°	measures more than 90°	measures exactly 180°

150°... OBTUSE! WHAM

Classify and write all possible names for each angle.

1.
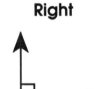

2.
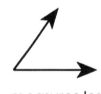

3.

4.
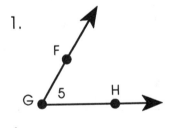

5.
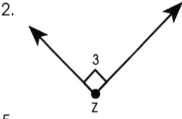
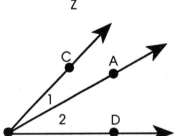

6.
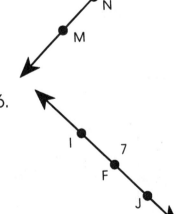

4

Light the Way

How long does it take for light from the sun to reach Earth?

To find out, complete the statements below. Then, write the corresponding letter above its answer at the bottom of the page.

(T) The intersection of the two sides of an angle is called the _____ .

(N) ∠BOE is a _____ angle.

(E) The figure formed by two rays with the same endpoint is an _____ .

(E) Another name for ∠3 is _____ .

(M) A _____ angle measures _____ .

(I) Another name for ∠COE is _____ .

(U) ∠AOD is an _____ angle.

(T) A right angle measures _____ .

(S) ∠BOC is a _____ angle.

(G) Another name for ∠AOD is _____ .

(H) ∠FOC is an _____ angle.

(I) Two rays that form an angle are called the _____ of the angle.

angle	∠2	∠4	acute	vertex		180°	sides	right	obtuse	90°	∠AOF	straight

5

Using a Protractor

Measuring Angles

∠ABC = 90°

1. Place the center mark of the protractor on the vertex of the angle (B).

2. Place the zero mark on one of the rays (B⃗A).

3. Use the scale to find the measure of the angle.

Drawing Angles

1. First, draw a ray with the straight edge of the protractor.

2. Place the center mark on point A and the zero mark on the ray.

3. Mark the desired degree (45°).

4. Use the straight edge of the protractor to connect the mark with the vertex.

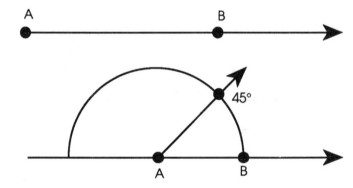

Using a protractor, measure the following angles.

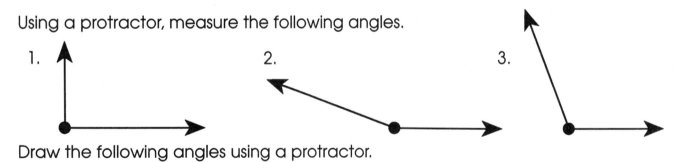

1.   2.   3.

Draw the following angles using a protractor.

4. 110°   5. 45°   6. 93°

The Freedom Trail

This map of the Freedom Trail in Boston, Massachusetts, shows several tourist attractions. Use it to answer the questions below.

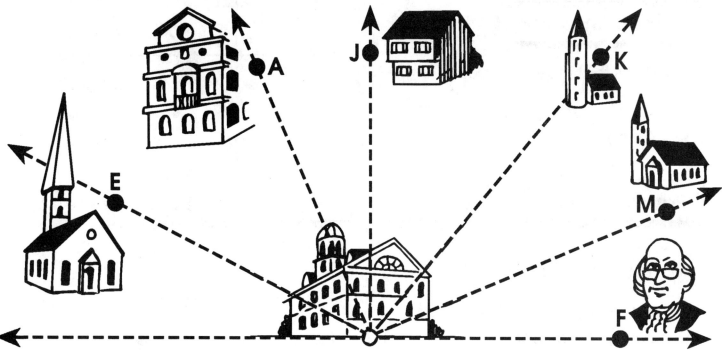

Using a protractor, find the measure (m) of each angle.

1. m∠EOJ = _____
2. m∠JOM = _____
3. m∠AOE = _____
4. m∠KOA = _____
5. m∠FOJ = _____

6. m∠FOA = _____
7. m∠MOK = _____
8. m∠MOE = _____
9. m∠EOF = _____
10. m∠KOE = _____

11. m∠AOJ = _____
12. m∠MOA = _____
13. m∠JOK = _____
14. m∠KOF = _____
15. m∠MOF = _____

Using a protractor, draw the measure of each angle.

16. 28°

18. 115°

20. 63°

17. 180°

19. 95°

21. 125°

Parallel, Perpendicular and Intersecting Lines

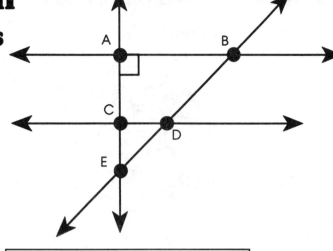

Intersecting Lines

two lines that meet at a point

$$\overleftrightarrow{AE} \text{ intersects } \overleftrightarrow{BE}$$

Line AE intersects line BE at point E.

Parallel Lines ‖

two lines that go in the same direction and never intersect

$$\overleftrightarrow{AB} \, \| \, \overleftrightarrow{CD}$$

Line AB is parallel to line CD.

Perpendicular Lines ⊥

two lines that intersect to form right angles

$$\overleftrightarrow{AE} \perp \overleftrightarrow{AB}$$

Line AE is perpendicular to line AB.

Use the figure below to answer the following questions.

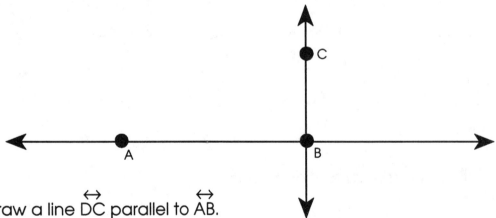

1. Draw a line $\overleftrightarrow{DC}$ parallel to $\overleftrightarrow{AB}$.

2. Draw a line intersecting $\overleftrightarrow{AB}$ and $\overleftrightarrow{DC}$. Make it perpendicular to $\overleftrightarrow{AB}$.

3. Draw a line intersecting $\overleftrightarrow{AB}$ and $\overleftrightarrow{DC}$ but not perpendicular to either one.

4. Name all parallel lines.

5. Name all perpendicular lines.

8

Following Directions

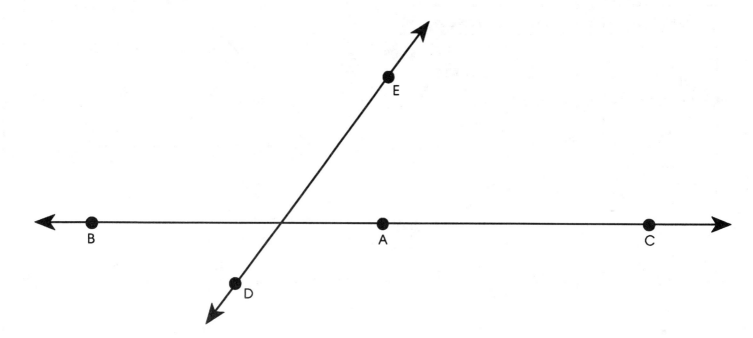

Follow the directions using the figure.

1. Draw a line $\overleftrightarrow{FG}$ parallel to $\overleftrightarrow{DE}$ and intersecting $\overleftrightarrow{BC}$.

2. Draw a ray $\overrightarrow{EH}$ extending from point E and going east. Make it parallel to $\overleftrightarrow{BC}$.

3. Draw a line $\overleftrightarrow{IJ}$ perpendicular to $\overleftrightarrow{AC}$ and intersecting $\overrightarrow{EH}$.

4. Draw a line $\overleftrightarrow{KL}$ intersecting $\overleftrightarrow{BC}$ but not perpendicular or parallel to any line.

5. Draw a line $\overleftrightarrow{MN}$ perpendicular to $\overleftrightarrow{DE}$.

Answer the questions using the figure.

6. What is parallel to $\overleftrightarrow{BA}$? _____

7. What line(s) is perpendicular to $\overleftrightarrow{BA}$? _____

8. What line(s) is parallel to $\overleftrightarrow{DE}$? _____

9. What line(s) is perpendicular to $\overleftrightarrow{DE}$? _____

10. Is $\overleftrightarrow{KL}$ parallel or perpendicular to any lines? _____

Classifying Triangles

Example	Name	Description
	acute	3 acute angles (angles less than 90°)
	obtuse	1 obtuse angle (angle greater than 90°)
	right	1 right angle (a 90° angle)
	scalene	no equal sides
	isosceles	2 equal sides
	equilateral	3 equal sides

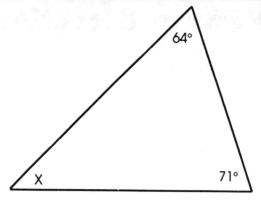

Find x.

Example 1

$$64° + 71° = 135°$$
$$180° — 135° = 45°$$
$$x = 45°$$

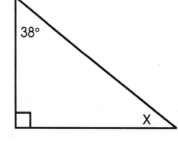

Example 2

$$90° + 38° = 128°$$
$$180° — 128° = 52°$$
$$x = 52°$$

*The sum of the measures of any triangle is 180°.

Give two names for each triangle and find x.

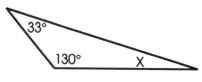

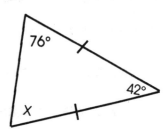

1. _____
2. _____
    x = _____

1. _____
2. _____
    x = _____

1. _____
2. _____
    x = _____

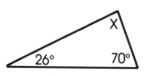

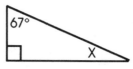

1. _____
2. _____
    x = _____

1. _____
2. _____
    x = _____

1. _____
2. _____
    x = _____

10

Tri These Angles!

Identify each triangle in the puzzle below by writing in the code letters from the box. Identify only the small triangles, not the ones made from smaller ones.

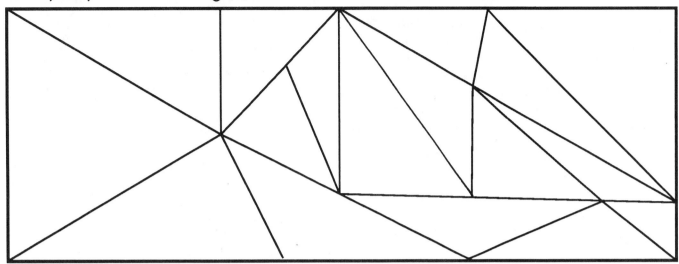

acute; scalene = AS	obtuse; scalene = OS	right; scalene = RS
acute; isosceles = AI	obtuse; isosceles = OI	right; isosceles = RI
acute; equilateral = AE		

What part of your body contains a hammer and an anvil?

To find out, find each missing angle measure. Write the angle above its measure at the bottom.

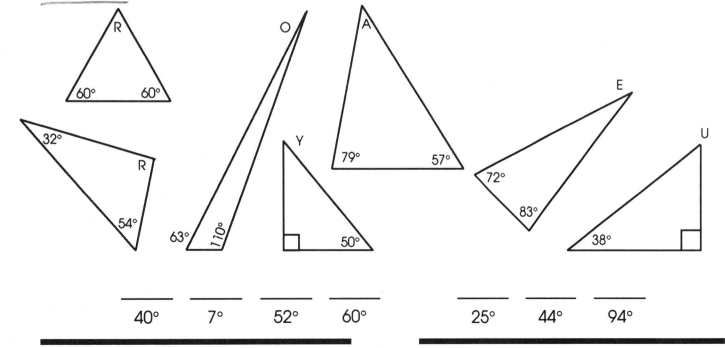

40°	7°	52°	60°		25°	44°	94°

11

Classifying Quadrilaterals

Name	Description	Example
trapezoid	1 pair of opposite sides parallel	
parallelogram	• opposite sides parallel • opposite sides and opposite angles congruent	
rhombus	parallelogram with all sides congruent	
rectangle	parallelogram with four right angles	
square	rectangle with four congruent sides	

*The sum of the measures of the angles in any quadrilateral is 360°.

Find x.

Example 1

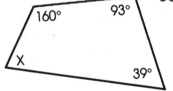

$$93° + 39° + 160° = 292°$$
$$360° - 292° = 68°$$
$$x = 68°$$

Example 2

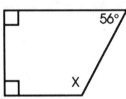

$$90° + 90° + 56° = 236°$$
$$360° - 236° = 124°$$
$$x = 124°$$

Give all the names for each quadrilateral. Then, find each missing angle measure.

1.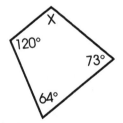

2.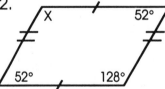

3.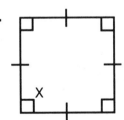

4.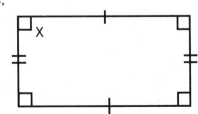

5.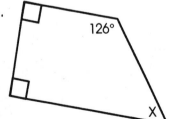

6.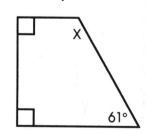

Woodpecker's Delight

Why does a woodpecker peck wood?

To find out, circle all the true statements beside each figure. Then, unscramble the letters to make a word. Write the words in order (going from left to right) in the boxes.

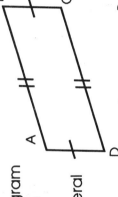
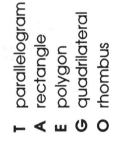
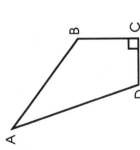
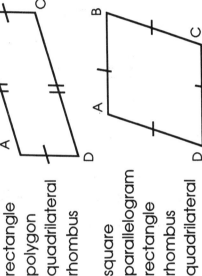
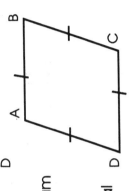
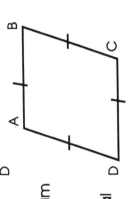
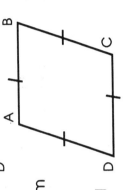
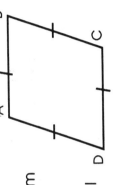

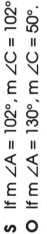
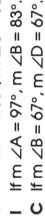
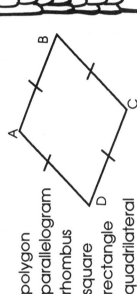

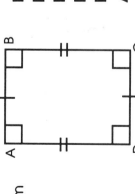
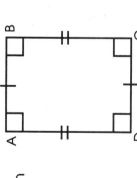

Figure (top left)
- G parallelogram
- A rectangle
- O polygon
- E square
- T quadrilateral

Figure (middle left)
- L parallelogram
- M square
- A rectangle
- O trapezoid
- L quadrilateral
- I m $\angle A = 75°$
- S m $\angle A = 90°$

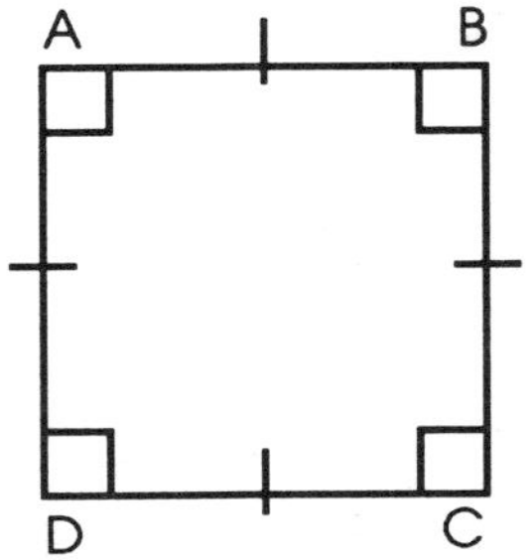

Figure (bottom left)
- E parallelogram
- A rhombus
- T rectangle
- O square
- H m $\angle A = 90°$
- E m $\angle A \neq 90°$

Figure (top middle)
- T parallelogram
- A rectangle
- E polygon
- G quadrilateral
- O rhombus

Figure (middle)
- A square
- E parallelogram
- T rectangle
- N rhombus
- T quadrilateral
- S polygon
- S If m $\angle A = 102°$, m $\angle C = 102°$.
- O If m $\angle A = 130°$, m $\angle C = 50°$.
- I If m $\angle A = 97°$, m $\angle B = 83°$.
- C If m $\angle B = 67°$, m $\angle D = 67°$.

Figure (bottom middle)
- K polygon
- B parallelogram
- R rhombus
- I square
- E rectangle
- A quadrilateral

Figure (top right)
- T parallelogram
- G square
- O rectangle
- M trapezoid
- A rhombus

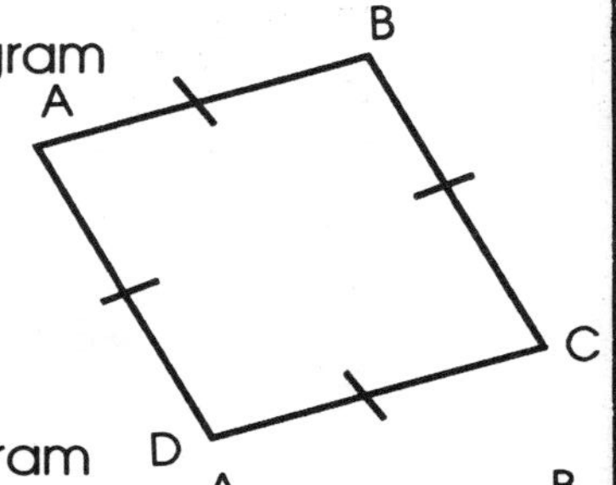

Figure (middle right)
- T parallelogram
- B quadrilateral
- N polygon
- M rhombus
- A trapezoid
- T m $\angle B = 90°$
- A m $\angle B \neq 90°$
- E If m $\angle A = 32°$, m $\angle D = 148°$.
- O If m $\angle A = 42°$, m $\angle D = 140°$.
- E If m $\angle D = 120°$, m $\angle A = 60°$.
- H If m $\angle D = 136°$, m $\angle A = 44°$.

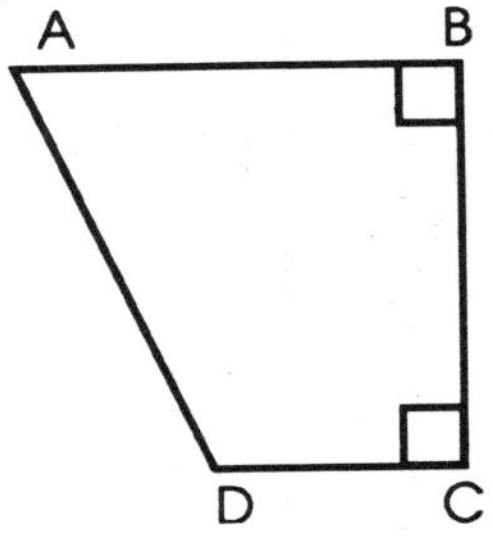

13

Polyhedrons

| **Polyhedron** | a space figure that has many faces that are flat and shaped like polygons |

Parts of a Polyhedron

Faces   flat surfaces (sides)

$$F = 4$$

Vertices   corners or points
(where 3 edges meet)

$$V = 4$$

Edges   parts of a line
(where 2 faces meet)

$$E = 6$$

Use this formula to tell if your space figure is a polyhedron.

$$E = F + V - 2$$

Example

$$6 = 4 + 4 - 2$$
$$8 - 2$$
$$6 = 6$$

Find the following parts of the space figures and tell if they are polyhedrons.

1.   F = _____
    V = _____
    E = _____
    E = F + V − 2

    Yes _____   No _____

2.   F = _____
    V = _____
    E = _____
    E = F + V − 2

    Yes _____   No _____

3.   F = _____
    V = _____
    E = _____
    E = F + V − 2

    Yes _____   No _____

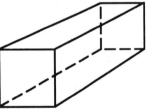

4.   F = _____
    V = _____
    E = _____
    E = F + V − 2

    Yes _____   No _____

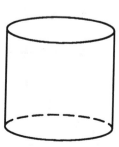

What a Bill!

What bird's bill may grow as long as its entire body?

To find out, follow the directions below using the following figures.

Figure 1 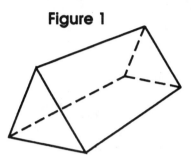 **Figure 2** 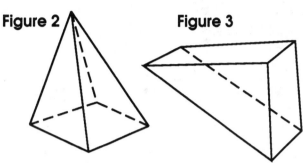 **Figure 3** **Figure 4**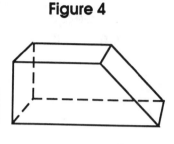

1. If the edges on Figure 1 equal 9, put an E above number 3.

2. If the faces on Figure 1 equal 4, put an E above number 2.

3. If the vertices on Figure 2 equal 6, put an O above number 6.

4. If the edges on Figure 4 equal 12, put a C above number 7.

5. If the vertices on Figure 3 equal 6, put an H above number 2.

6. If the faces on Figure 3 equal 5, put an O above number 5.

7. If the faces on Figure 4 equal 7, put an A above number 7.

8. If the edges on Figure 3 equal 9, put an A above number 8.

9. If the faces on Figure 2 equal 5, put a T above number 1.

10. If the edges on Figure 1 equal 10, put an E above number 9.

11. If the faces on Figure 4 equal 6, put a U above number 6.

12. If the vertices on Figure 4 equal 8, put an S above number 10.

13. If the edges on Figure 3 equal 10, put a T above number 3.

14. If the edges on Figure 2 equal 8, put an N above number 9.

15. If the vertices on Figure 1 equal 6, put a T above number 4.

___ ___ ___   ___ ___   ___ ___ ___ ___ ___
 1   2   3   4   5   6   7   8   9   10

Graphing Ordered Pairs

Ordered Pair (x, y)

The first number, x, tells the number of units to the right of 0.

The second number, y, tells the number of units up from 0.

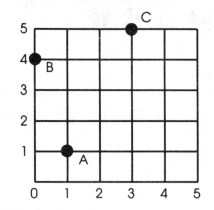

Point	Ordered Pair	Description
A	(1, 1)	1 unit right, 1 unit up
B	(0, 4)	0 units right, 4 units up
C	(3, 5)	3 units right, 5 units up

Graph each point on the graph below.

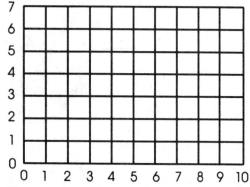

1. S (2, 5)   5. G (0, 0)

2. X (0, 3)   6. M (6, 3)

3. C (1, 2)   7. J (4, 0)

4. T (5, 5)   8. A (3, 4)

Write the ordered pair for each point on the graph below.

1. M   5. S

2. B   6. K

3. Y   7. C

4. N   8. G

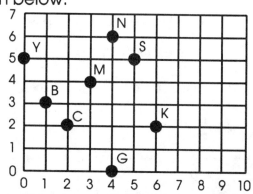

16

What Am I?

Graph the following ordered pairs. Connect the points in order and give all the names of the polygons.

(6, 5)
(5, 2)
(1, 2)
(2, 5)
(6, 5)

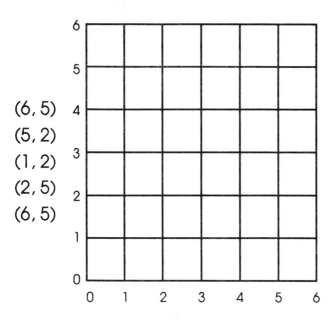

(2, 4)
(5, 4)
(6, 1)
(0, 1)
(2, 4)

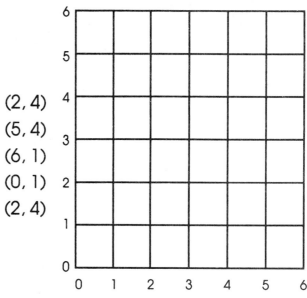

(2, 3)
(2, 6)
(5, 8)
(8, 6)
(8, 3)
(5, 1)
(2, 3)

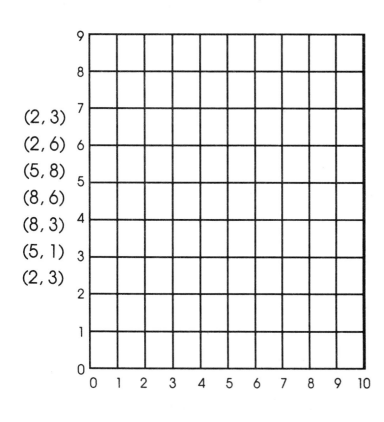

(2, 1)
(2, 4)
(5, 1)
(5, 4)
(2, 1)

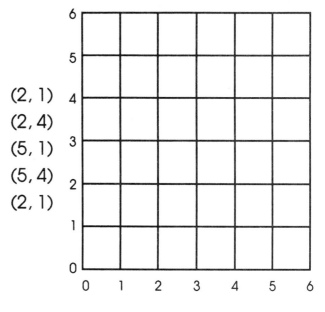

Polygons

17

Area of Parallelograms

Area of a Parallelogram

the length times the width

$$A = l \times w$$

- The length (20 cm) is how long the figure is.
- The width (12 cm) is how wide the figure is.

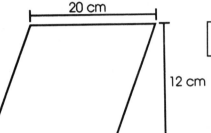

20 cm

Example 1

$$A = l(20) \times w(12)$$
$$A = 20 \times 12$$
$$A = 240 \text{ cm}^2$$

Area is measured in square units.

12 cm

Example 2

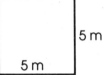

5 m

5 m

$$A = 5 \times 5$$
$$A = 25 \text{ m}^2$$

Since a square has the same length and width, the area is side times side.
$$A = s \times s = s^2$$

Example 3

Divide the figure into rectangles. Find the area of each rectangle. Then, add the areas together to find the total area.

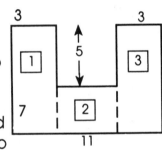

3   3

1   5   3

7   7

2   11

A1 = 7 x 3 = 21 mm²
A2 = 5 x 2 = 10 mm²
A3 = 7 x 3 = 21 mm²
21 + 10 + 21 = 52 mm²

Find the area of each figure.

1.

8
8

2.
21
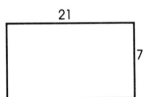
7

3.
16
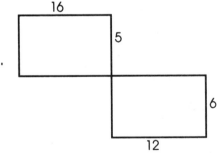
5
6
12

Find the area of the shaded region.

4.
16 m
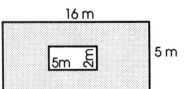
5 m
5m   2m

5.
20   26
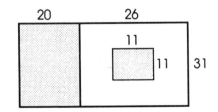
11
11   31

Randy the Robot

Find the area of each parallelogram that makes up the robot.

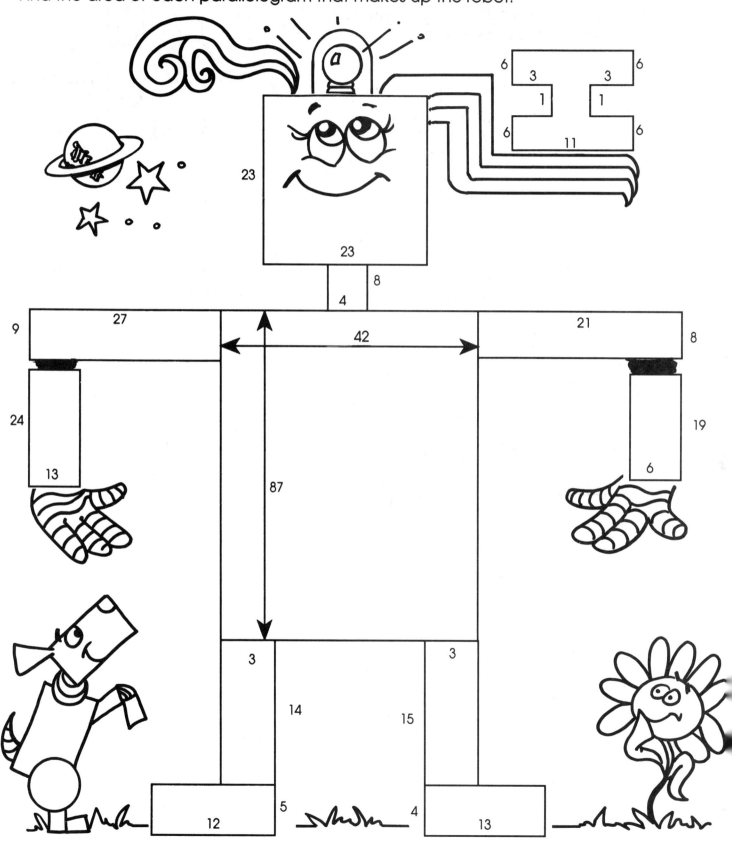

Area of Triangles

Area of a Triangle

one half the base times the height

$A = \frac{1}{2} \times b \times h$

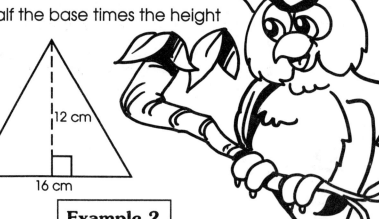

- The base (16 cm) is the length of the bottom of the figure.
- The height (12 cm) is the length of the height of the figure.

12 cm

16 cm

Example 1

$A = \frac{1}{2} \times b(16) \times h(12)$

$A = \frac{1}{2} \times 16 \times 12$

$A = 96 \text{ cm}^2$

Area is measured in square units.

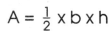

Example 2

$A = \frac{1}{2} \times 36 \times 8.9$

(Hint: $\frac{1}{2} = .5$)

$A = .5 \times 36 \times 8.9$

$A = 160.2 \text{ m}^2$

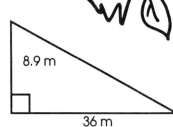

8.9 m

36 m

Example 3

Find the area of the figure.

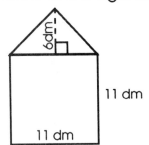

6 dm

11 dm

11 dm

Find the area of each section. Then, add all the areas together to find the total area.

Area of triangle = $\frac{1}{2} \times 11 \times 6$

$A = 33 \text{ dm}^2$

Area of square = 11×11

$A = 121 \text{ dm}^2$

$33 + 121 = 154 \text{ dm}^2$

Find the area of each figure.

1.

6.7 m

5.2 m

A = _____

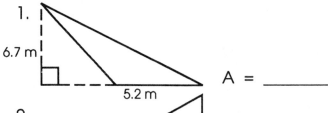

2.

11 mm

27 mm

A = _____

3.

12 dam

12 dam

6 m

A = _____

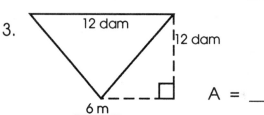

4.

8 m   26 m   26 m   8 m

A = _____

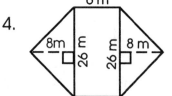

Rocky Road

What is the only type of rock that can float?

To find out, find the areas of the following triangles at the bottom of the page and put the corresponding letter above each answer. Note: Some answers may not be given.

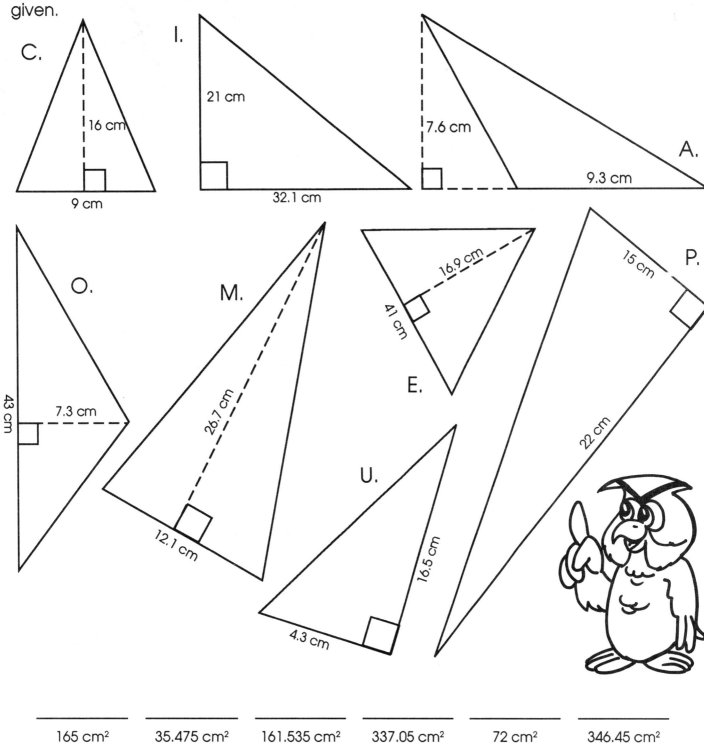

C. 16 cm 9 cm

I. 21 cm 32.1 cm

A. 7.6 cm 9.3 cm

O. 43 cm 7.3 cm

M. 26.7 cm 12.1 cm

E. 41 cm 16.9 cm

P. 15 cm 22 cm

U. 16.5 cm 4.3 cm

| 165 cm² | 35.475 cm² | 161.535 cm² | 337.05 cm² | 72 cm² | 346.45 cm² |

21

Circumference of Circles

Circumference

distance around the circle

$C = \pi \times d$

π (pi) ≈ 3.14 or $\frac{22}{7}$ ($\approx$ means approximately equal to)

d = diameter

Use $\pi \approx 3.14$ and round to the nearest one.

Example 1

$C = \pi(3.14) \times d(8.6)$

$C \approx 3.14 \times 8.6$

$C \approx 27.004$ km

$C \approx 27$ km

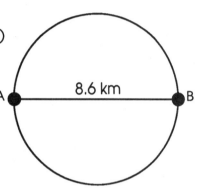

A   8.6 km   B

Example 2

16 is equal to radius. Diameter is twice the radius. So, d = 16 x 2 = 32.

$C \approx 3.14 \times 32$

$C \approx 100.48$ mm

$C \approx 100$ mm

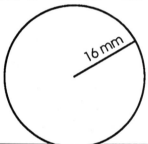

16 mm

Example 3

Find the perimeter of the figure.

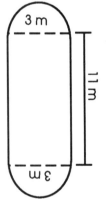

3 m

11 m

3 m

Circumference of circle =
   $3.14 \times 3 = 9.42$ m

   $9.42 + 11 + 11 = 31.42$ m

Find the circumference of each circle. Use $\pi = 3.14$ and round to the nearest one.

1.   2.   3.   4.

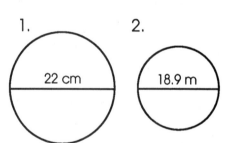

22 cm   18.9 m

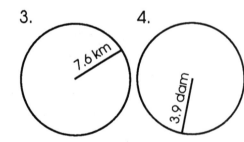

7.6 km   3.9 dam

Find the perimeter of each figure.

5.   6.

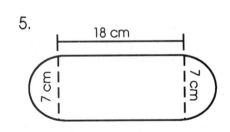

18 cm

7 cm   7 cm

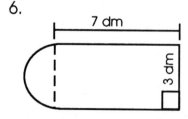

7 dm

3 dm

Alex the Anteater

Help Alex the Anteater get to his dinner by finding the correct path. Shade in the path of the circumferences that are true. Then, find the correct circumferences for the ones that are wrong.

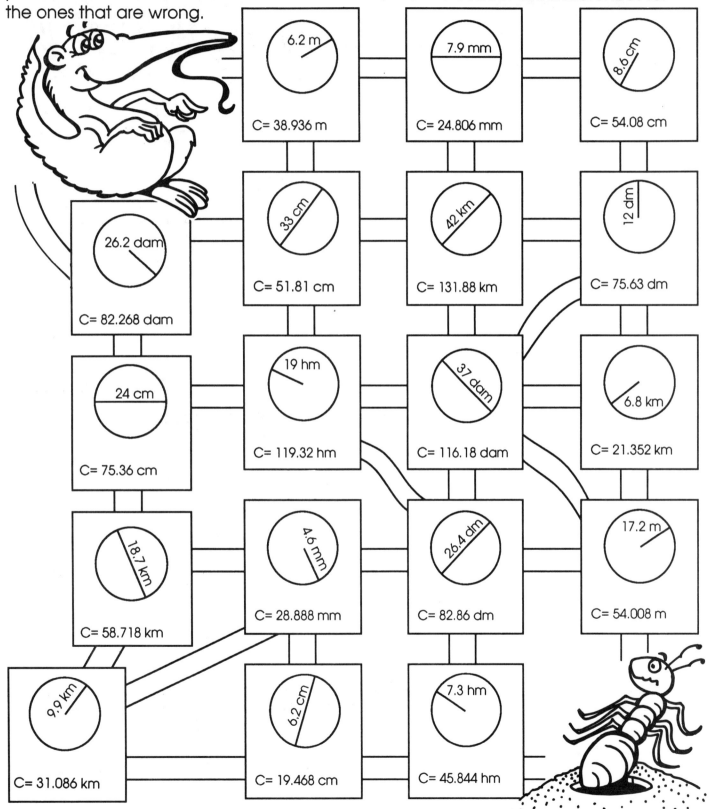

23

Area of Circles

Area of a Circle

pi times the radius squared

$A = \pi \times r^2 \; (r^2 = r \times r)$

$\pi \approx 3.14$ or $\frac{22}{7}$

Use $\pi \approx 3.14$ and round to the nearest one.

Example 1

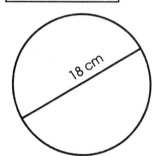

$A = \pi(3.14) \times r^2 (7 \times 7)$

$A \approx 3.14 \times 7 \times 7$

$A \approx 153.86 \; m^2$

$A \approx 154 \; m^2$

Area is measured in square units.

7m

Example 2

18 = diameter

radius = 1/2 diameter

r = 18 ÷ 2 = 9

$A \approx 3.14 \times 9^2$

$A \approx 254.34 \; cm^2$

$A \approx 254 \; cm^2$

18 cm

Example 3

Find the area of the shaded region.

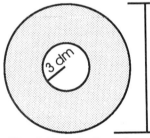

3 dm

26 dm

Area of larger circle $\approx 3.14 \times 13^2 \; (r = 26 \div 2)$

$A \approx 530.66 \; dm^2$

$A \approx 531 \; dm^2$

Area of smaller circle $\approx 3.14 \times 3^2$

$A \approx 28.26 \; dm^2$

$A \approx 28 \; dm^2$

Area of shaded region = 531 − 28 = 503 dm^2

Find the following areas. Use $\pi = 3.14$ and round to the nearest one.

1.
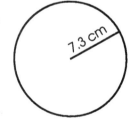
7.3 cm

2.
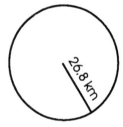
26.8 km

3.
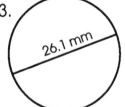
26.1 mm

4.
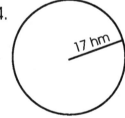
17 hm

Find the area of each shaded region.

5.
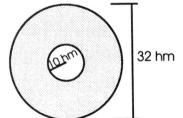
10 hm
32 hm

6.
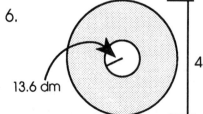
13.6 dm
43 dm

No Bones About It!

What part of your body contains one quarter of all of your bones?

To find out, find the area (rounded to the nearest one) of each circle or shaded region below. Then, write the corresponding letter of the problem above the answer at the bottom of the page.

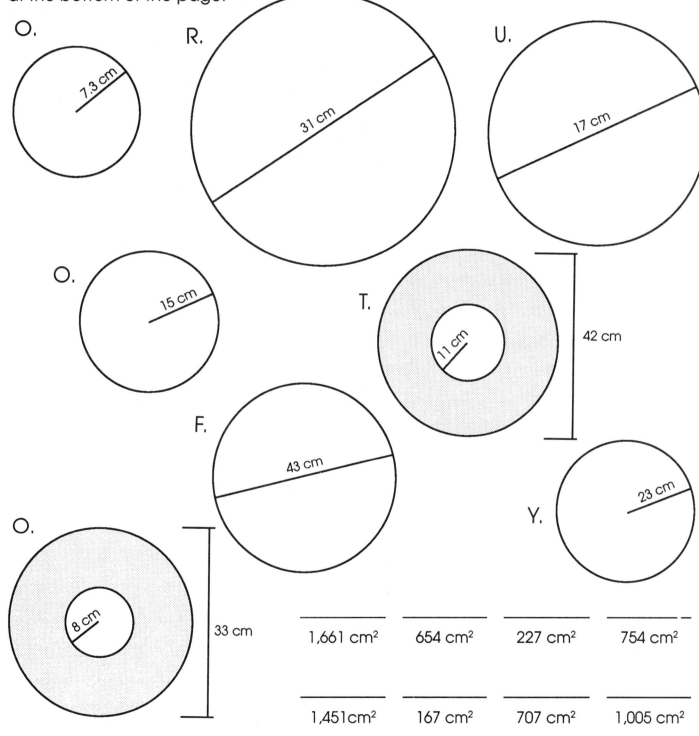

O.
7.3 cm

R.
31 cm

U.
17 cm

O.
15 cm

T.
11 cm
42 cm

F.
43 cm

Y.
23 cm

O.
8 cm
33 cm

1,661 cm²	654 cm²	227 cm²	754 cm²

| 1,451cm² | 167 cm² | 707 cm² | 1,005 cm² |

25

$+¢-×÷=$+¢-×÷=$+¢-×÷=$+¢-×÷=$

Relating Customary Units of Length

Example 1   5 mi = _____ yd

To change from a larger unit to a smaller unit, multiply. You multiply because you expect a larger number.

1 mi = 1,760 yd

5 x 1,760 = 8,800

5 mi = 8,800 yd

Length
1 foot (ft) = 12 inches (in.)
1 yard (yd) = 36 inches
1 yard = 3 feet
1 mile (mi) = 5,280 feet
1 mile = 1,760 yards

Example 2   7,040 yd = _____ mi

To change from a smaller unit to a larger unit, divide. You divide because you expect a smaller number.

1,760 yd = 1 mi

7,040 ÷ 1,760 = 4

7,040 yd = 4 mi

Example 3   162 in. = _____ yd

36 in. = 1 yd

162 ÷ 36 = 4 R18

When you have a remainder, you express it in the original unit, ex: in.

162 in. = 4 yd 18 in.

Complete.

1. 144 in. = _____ ft

2. 96 ft = _____ yd

3. 7 mi = _____ ft

4. 81 yd = _____ in.

5. 14,080 yd = _____ mi

6. 48 ft = _____ in.

Circle the larger distance.

7. 42 in.   or   3 ft

8. 8 ft   or   3 yd

9. 7 mi   or   12,300 yd

Puzzling Lengths

Write the word form of the answers in the puzzle.

Across

3. 7 yd = _____ in.

6. 31,680 ft = _____ mi

8. 290 in. = _____ yd 2 in.

9. 15,840 ft = _____ mi

11. 8 yd = _____ ft

12. Which is larger: 8 yd or 22 ft?

13. 6,281 yd = _____ mi 1,001 yd

14. 92 in. = _____ ft 8 in.

15. Which is larger: 42 in. or 4 ft?

Down

1. 14,080 yd = _____ mi

2. 20 ft = 6 yd _____ ft

3. 90 ft = _____ yd

4. 228 in. = _____ ft

5. 7 ft = _____ in.

7. 540 in. = _____ yd

10. Which is larger: 11 mi or 19,300 yd?

Relating Customary Units of Weight and Capacity

Example 1	$5\,T = \underline{\hspace{1cm}}$ lb

To change from a larger unit to a smaller unit, multiply.

$1\,T = 2{,}000$ lb

$5 \times 2{,}000 = 10{,}000$

$5\,T = 10{,}000$ lb

Weight
1 pound (lb) = 16 ounces (oz)
1 ton (T) = 2,000 pounds

Example 2	176 fl oz $= \underline{\hspace{1cm}}$ c

To change from a smaller unit to a larger unit, divide.

8 fl oz $= 1$ c

$176 \div 8 = 22$

176 fl oz $= 22$ c

Capacity
1 cup (c) = 8 fluid ounces (fl oz)
1 pint (pt) = 2 cups
1 quart (qt) = 2 pints
1 gallon (gal) = 4 quarts

Example 3	$25\,c = \underline{\hspace{1cm}}$ pt

$2\,c = 1$ pt

$25 \div 2 = 12$ R1

Express remainders in terms of the original unit.

$25\,c = 12$ pt 1 c

Complete.

1. 16 pt $= \underline{\hspace{1cm}}$ qt

2. 12 gal $= \underline{\hspace{1cm}}$ qt

3. 5 lb $= \underline{\hspace{1cm}}$ oz

4. 150 oz $= \underline{\hspace{1cm}}$ lb $\underline{\hspace{1cm}}$ oz

5. 5 gal 3 qt $= \underline{\hspace{1cm}}$ qt

6. 2 lb 3 oz $= \underline{\hspace{1cm}}$ oz

Compare using >, <, =.

7. 1 gal 6 qt

8. 560 oz 35 lb

9. 15 pt 25 c

28

Go Genie Go!

Help the Genie get back to his lamp by shading in the true equations to form a path. Then, find the correct answers to the ones that are wrong.

8 c = 64 fl oz	71 qt > 285 c	417 fl oz = 26 pt	22 pt = 11 qt 1 pt	21 T = 44,000 lb
7 pt = 14 c	18 lb = 289 oz	11 qt = 22 pt	96 fl oz = 12 c	86 pt = 43 qt
17 gal = 272 c	8 gal 2 qt = 35 qt	160,000 oz = 5 T	68 oz < 4 lb	11 gal = 88 pt
23 pt = 368 fl oz	15 qt = 62 c	8 gal = 32 qt	7 gal = 115 c	224,000 oz = 7 T
31 pt > 60 c	29 lb = 460 oz	25 lb = 400 oz	540 oz = 34 lb	16 pt = 256 fl oz
3 T = 6,000 lb	515 fl oz = 4 gal	11 gal > 81 pt	50 c = 12 qt 3 c	46 c = 23 pt
35 qt = 140 c	410 oz = 25 lb 11 oz	204 qt = 51 gal	130 pt = 16 gal	
11 T = 22,000 lb	11 pt = 176 fl oz	72 c = 18 qt	12 T = 25,000 lb	
26 gal = 200 pt	193,000 oz = 6 T	15 gal = 241 c	70 c = 18 qt	

Relating Metric Units of Length

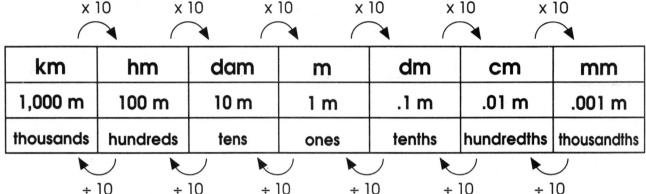

km	hm	dam	m	dm	cm	mm
1,000 m	100 m	10 m	1 m	.1 m	.01 m	.001 m
thousands	hundreds	tens	ones	tenths	hundredths	thousandths

kilometer (km)
hectometer (hm)
dekameter (dam)
meter (m)
decimeter (dm)
centimeter (cm)
millimeter (mm)

Example 1   2.3 dm = _____ mm

To change to a smaller unit, multiply by 10 for each box you move to the right. (Move the decimal point one place to the right for each box.)

Decimeters to millimeters is two boxes to the right. Multiply by 100.

2.3 x 100 = 230
2.3 dm = 230 mm

Example 2   5 dm = _____ hm

To change to a larger unit, divide by 10 for each box you move to the left. (Move the decimal point one place to the left for each box.)

Decimeters to hectometers is three boxes to the left. Divide by 1,000.

5 ÷ 1,000 = .005
5 dm = .005 hm

Solve using the chart above.

1. 80 km = _____ dm

2. 16 mm = _____ dm

3. 12.1 m = _____ mm

4. 7.1 hm = _____ cm

5. 4.6 dam = _____ dm

6. .01 hm = _____ mm

7. 5.32 hm = _____ m

8. .01 dm = _____ km

9. 9 cm = _____ dam

Bull's Eye

Use the chart to help you fill in the targets. Each target will have different units for the rings.

km	hm	dam	m	dm	cm	mm
1,000 m	100 m	10 m	1 m	.1 m	.01 m	.001 m

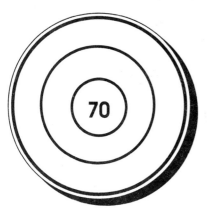

center = mm
middle = dm
outside = dam

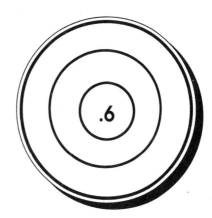

center = dam
middle = km
outside = cm

center = dm
middle = m
outside = mm

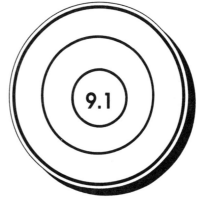

center = m
middle = mm
outside = hm

center = hm
middle = km
outside = cm

center = cm
middle = m
outside = hm

Relating Metric Units of Mass (Weight) and Capacity

	x 10	x 10	x 10	x 10	x 10	x 10
kg	hg	dag	g	dg	cg	mg
kL	hL	daL	L	dL	cL	mL
1,000	100	10	1	.1	.01	.001
thousands	hundreds	tens	ones	tenths	hundredths	thousandths

÷ 10   ÷ 10   ÷ 10   ÷ 10   ÷ 10   ÷ 10

kilogram (kg)   decigram (dg)   kiloliter (kL)   deciliter (dL)
hectogram (hg)   centigram (cg)   hectoliter (hL)   centiliter (cL)
dekagram (dag)   milligram (mg)   dekaliter (daL)   milliliter (mL)
gram (g)   liter (L)

Example 1   .06 dag = _____ cg

To change to a smaller unit, multiply by 10 for each box you move to the right. (Move the decimal point one place to the right for each box.)

Dekagrams to centigrams is three boxes to the right. Multiply by 1,000.

.06 x 1,000 = 60
.06 dag = 60 cg

Example 2   81 dL = _____ kL

To change to a larger unit, divide by 10 for each box you move to the left. (Move the decimal point one place to the left for each box.)

Deciliters to kiloliters is four boxes to the left. Divide by 10,000.

81 ÷ 10,000 = .0081
81 dL = .0081 kL

Solve using the chart above.

1. 16 dg = _____ mg

2. 6.1 mL = _____ hL

3. 16.8 hL = _____ cL

4. 8.9 dag = _____ dg

5. 16 kg = _____ g

6. 9 L = _____ hL

7. .08 cL = _____ L

8. 9 g = _____ mg

9. .06 hg = _____ mg

An Amazing Animal

What African animal is born under water and swims before it walks?

To find out, solve the problems on the left. Draw a straight line connecting the problem to its answer. The line should pass through a letter and a number. Put the letter above the box with the correct answer at the bottom of the page.

41 dL = _____ hL ❑ ⑦

7.2 kg = _____ dg ❑ ⑬

11.01 g = _____ mg ❑

21.6 cL = _____ daL ❑

7 cL = _____ hL ❑

16.013 kg = _____ dag ❑

.062 g = _____ cg ❑

310 hg = _____ g ❑

210 mL = _____ L ❑

.013 cL = _____ hL ❑

21.9 daL = _____ kL ❑

11 L = _____ hL ❑

.121 cg = _____ dag ❑

11.61 hL = _____ dL ❑

29.6 mg = _____ g ❑

Ⓔ
Ⓜ
Ⓟ
Ⓞ
③
⑤
②
Ⓣ
Ⓢ
Ⓟ
⑨
⑩
Ⓘ
⑥
⑮
⑫
Ⓐ
①
Ⓞ
Ⓤ
⑭
Ⓟ
⑧
Ⓗ
Ⓣ
⑪
Ⓗ
④

❑ 1601.3

❑ .11

❑ 72,000

❑ .0216

❑ .0000013

❑ .041

❑ 6.2

❑ 11,610

❑ .21

❑ 11,010

❑ .219

❑ 31,000

❑ .0296

❑ .000121

❑ .007

1	2	3		4	5	6	7	8	9	10	11	12	13	14	15

Ratios

Ratios

a comparison
of two
quantities

Equal Ratios   To find equal ratios,
multiply or divide
both terms by the
same number.

Example   4:3   Name 2 equal fractions.

4:3 is $\frac{4}{3}$

$\frac{4}{3}$ (×3) $= \frac{12}{9}$ $\frac{4}{3}$ (×5) $= \frac{20}{15}$

Example   Find the ratio of bananas
to apples.

First, find how many bananas. 4
Then, find how many apples. 3
There are 4 bananas to 3 apples.
The ratio can be written in three ways.

4 to 3   4:3 $\frac{4}{3}$

Use the fruit basket above to find the ratios. Write each ratio three ways. Then, find
two equal ratios.

1. apples to grapes

    apples = _____

    grapes = _____

    __ to __ or __ : __ or __

2. oranges to apples

    oranges = _____

    apples = _____

    ____ or ____ or ____

3. grapes to bananas

    grapes = _____

    bananas = _____

    ____ or ____ or ____

4. apples to bananas

    apples = _____

    bananas = _____

    ____ or ____ or ____

5. bananas to oranges

    bananas = _____

    oranges = _____

    ____ or ____ or ____

6. oranges to grapes

    oranges = _____

    grapes = _____

    ____ or ____ or ____

34

Hhhmm?

What do the four H's stand for in the 4-H Club?

To find out, solve the following ratios. Find the answers at the bottom of the page. Put the corresponding problem letter above the answer. When you have answered the riddle, write each ratio two other ways and find two equivalent ratios for each one.

E. tennis shoes to sandals _____
N. bare feet to men's dress shoes _____
S. high heels to tennis shoes _____
E. sandals to bare feet _____
E. men's dress shoes to high heels _____
A. high heels to sandals _____
T. bare feet to tennis shoes _____
A. high heels to bare feet _____
D. tennis shoes to men's dress shoes _____
H. men's dress shoes to sandals _____
H. bare feet to sandals _____
R. sandals to high heels _____
H. tennis shoes to high heels _____
D. sandals to tennis shoes _____
T. men's dress shoes to tennis shoes _____
H. tennis shoes to bare feet _____
L. high heels to men's dress shoes _____
A. men's dress shoes to bare feet _____
A. bare feet to high heels _____
H. sandals to men's dress shoes _____

___ ___ ___ ___ ,   ___ ___ ___ ___ ___ ,
3:5 6:5 2:5 3:1   5:6 3:6 1:5 6:2 5:3

___ ___ ___ ___ ___ ___ ,   ___ ___ ___ ___ ___
1:6 1:2 5:2 2:1 1:3 6:1   3:2 2:6 5:1 6:3 2:3

35

$+¢-×÷=$+¢-×÷=$+¢-×÷=$+¢-×÷=$

Proportion

| **Proportion** | states that two ratios are equal. |

| **Example 1** | Is $\frac{8}{10} = \frac{4}{5}$ a proportion? |

To test for a proportion, use equal ratios or cross products.
In a proportion, cross products are equal.

Equal Ratios

$$\frac{8}{10} = \frac{4}{5}$$

$$\frac{8 (\div 2)}{10 (\div 2)} = \frac{4}{5}$$

Cross Products

$$\frac{8}{10} \bowtie \frac{4}{5}$$

$$8 \times 5 = 10 \times 4$$
$$40 = 40$$

The ratios are equal.

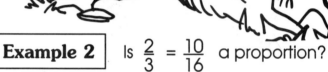

| **Example 2** | Is $\frac{2}{3} = \frac{10}{16}$ a proportion? |

$$2 \times 16 \boxed{} 3 \times 10$$
$$32 \neq 30$$
No.

Compare. Fill in each box with = or ≠ to make a true statement.

1. $\frac{5}{8} \boxed{} \frac{15}{24}$

2. $\frac{8}{9} \boxed{} \frac{24}{27}$

3. $\frac{6}{7} \boxed{} \frac{13}{14}$

4. $\frac{12}{14} \boxed{} \frac{18}{21}$

5. $\frac{9}{32} \boxed{} \frac{12}{64}$

6. $\frac{3}{15} \boxed{} \frac{7}{35}$

Sam the Squirrel

Help Sam the Squirrel get his acorns to his tree by shading in the path containing the correct proportions.

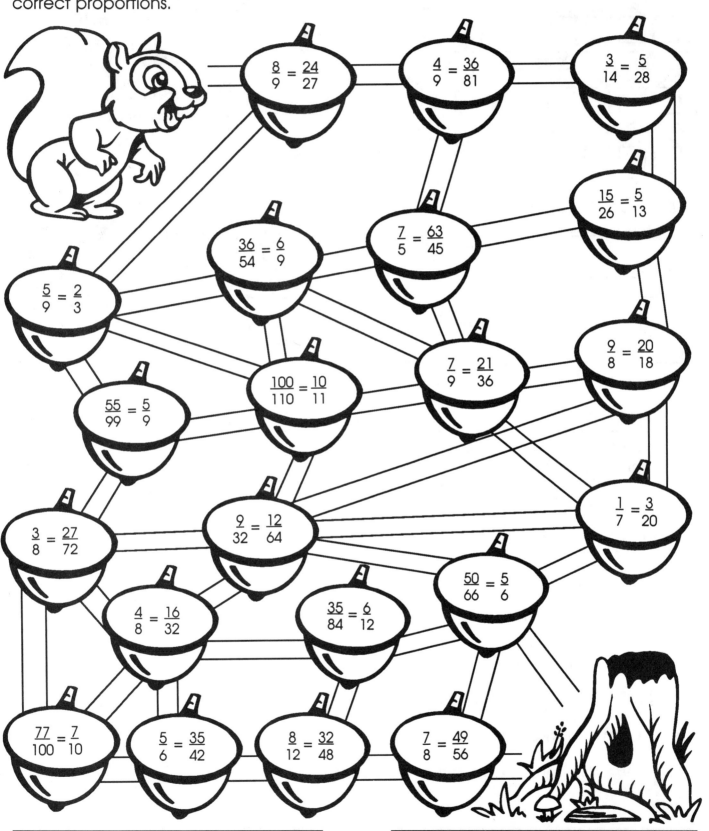

Map Scales

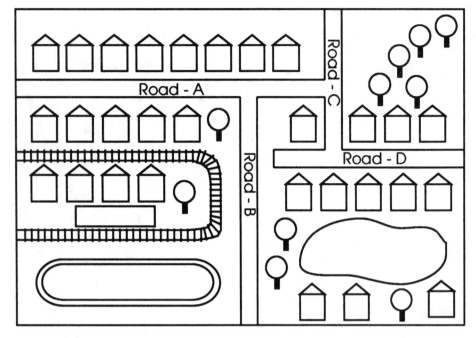

├──┤ 1 cm = 4 miles

Map Scales

are used to estimate distances on a map.

It compares the distance on a map with the actual distance.

This map has a scale of 1 to 4, or 1:4 or $\frac{1}{4}$.

| Example | How many miles long is Road A? |

1. Use a ruler to measure the distance on the map.

    9 cm

2. Write a proportion using the scale as a ratio.

    $\frac{scale}{actual}$ $\frac{1}{4} = \frac{9}{X}$

3. Solve the proportion.

    $\frac{1}{4} = \frac{9}{X}$

    $1 \times X = 4 \times 9$

    $X = 36$

    Road A is 36 miles long.

Use the map above to answer the following questions.

1. How many miles long is Road B? _____

2. How many miles long is Road C? _____

3. How many miles long is Road D? _____

4. How many miles long are the rainroad tracks? _____

Map It Out!

Make your own map using the map scale that is given.

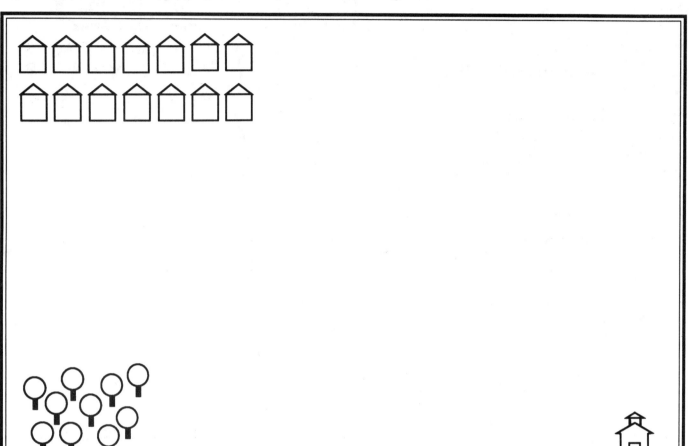

⊢———⊣ 1 cm = 2.5 miles

1. Draw a road 16 miles long going east to west between the park and the neighborhood. Label it Hill Road.

2. Draw a road 21 miles long going north to south starting from the schoolhouse. Label it Schoolhouse Drive.

3. Draw a road 18 miles long perpendicular to and intersecting Hill Road. Make sure it starts by the houses. Label it Neighborhood Road.

4. Draw a public swimming pool 24 miles northeast of the park.

5. Draw a playground 12 miles south of the swimming pool and 20 miles east of the park.

6. Draw a soccer field 27 miles east of the neighborhood.

7. Draw a fountain 11 miles northeast of the pool and 17.5 miles from the schoolhouse.

Mean, Median, Mode and Range

| Example | Jim had the following test scores in math: 100, 90, 68, 70, 80, 84, 100, 100, 100. Find the mean, median, mode and range of his scores. |

| **Mean** | same as average |

First, add up all the scores.

100 + 90 + 68 + 70 + 80 + 84 + 100 + 100 + 100 = 792

Then, divide by the number of tests.

$$792 ÷ 9 = \textbf{88}$$

| **Median** | the middle score |

First, arrange scores in order.

68, 70, 80, 84, 90, 100, 100, 100, 100

Then, find the middle number. **90**

(Hint: If there is not one middle number, add the two middle numbers and divide by two. Example: 2, 4, 5, 9)

4 + 5 = 9 9 ÷ 2 = **4.5**   4.5 is median.

| **Mode** | the score that occurs most often |

100

| **Range** | the difference between the highest and the lowest score |

100 − 68 = **32**

Find the mean, median, mode and range of each set of numbers.

1. 3, 4, 7, 3, 3, 4, 2, 3

mean _____

median _____

mode _____

range _____

2. 45, 45, 22, 18, 46, 31

mean _____

median _____

mode _____

range _____

3. 28, 26, 30, 28, 27, 29, 28

mean _____

median _____

mode _____

range _____

4. 150, 200, 150, 150, 210, 304, 173

mean _____

median _____

mode _____

range _____

Solar RM³

Find the range, median, mode, and mean of the numbers in the stars that are attached by stardust and put the answers in the shapes.

Mean, Median, Mode and Range

55, 63, 74, 70, 70, 64

73, 81, 67, 33, 33, 43

36, 38, 40, 50, 54, 40

11, 15, 12, 20, 15

8, 9, 8, 6, 10

6, 7, 6, 5, 3

Broken-Line, Bar and Circle Graphs

Data

time	heart rate
0 min.	80
5 min.	120
10 min.	135
15 min.	147
20 min.	159
25 min.	150

Broken-Line Graph

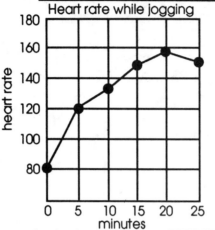

Bar Graph

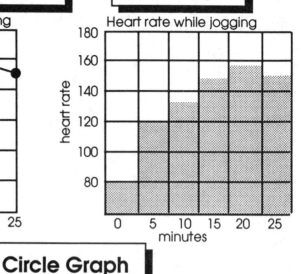

Organizing data into graphs helps people to understand the information by means of a quick, visual inspection.

To make a graph:

1. Label each scale (minutes and heart rate).
2. Create each scale to fit your data (0 to 25 and 80 to at least 160).
3. Plot your data.
4. Title your graph.

Circle Graph

Favorite Ice Cream Flavors

30% chocolate

20% other

12% mint

13% strawberry

25% vanilla

Remember: A circle graph must equal 100%.

On the back of the page, make a bar graph and a broken-line graph using the following information.

Month	Rainfall in inches
Jan.	1
Feb.	3
Mar.	7
April	15
May	11
June	4
July	8
Aug.	2
Sept.	9
Oct.	8
Nov.	3
Dec.	0

On the back of the page, make a circle graph using the following information.

Favorite Time for Study

after dinner	35%
after school	25%
before school	15%
during school	15%
other	10%

Graphs Galore!

Make each of the following graphs using the information given. Then, answer the questions using the graphs.

Broken-Line Graph

TEMPERATURES IN ST. LOUIS FOR ONE WEEK

Saturday	63°
Sunday	65°
Monday	61°
Tuesday	63°
Wednesday	70°
Thursday	68°
Friday	66°

Bar Graph

TOTAL NUMBER OF HITS FOR ONE SEASON

Sally	18
Sue	16
Jill	23
Mary	15
Lee	31
Janie	23
Judy	33

Circle Graph

SIXTH GRADERS' FAVORITE CLASS IN SCHOOL

Math	20%
History	10%
Science	30%
Reading	20%
Physical Ed.	10%
Music	5%
Art	5%

1. Who had the most number of hits in one season? _____

2. What day was the warmest? _____

3. What percent of sixth graders like math and music? _____

4. What day was the coldest? _____

5. What percent of sixth graders like science and art? _____

6. What two players had the same number of hits? _____

7. What is the difference between the highest and lowest temperatures? _____

8. What is the sixth graders' favorite class? _____

9. Who had the least number of hits in one season? _____

10. On what two days was the temperature 63°? _____

ANSWER KEY

Math Topics

Grade 6

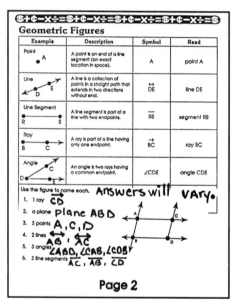

Geometric Figures

Example	Description	Symbol	Read
Point •A	A point is an end of a line segment (an exact location in space).	A	point A
Line D·—E	A line is a collection of points in a straight path that extends in two directions without end.	↔ DE	line DE
Line Segment R·—·S	A line segment is part of a line with two endpoints.	‾RS‾	segment RS
Ray B·—·C	A ray is part of a line having only one endpoint.	→ BC	ray BC
Angle D·—·C	An angle is two rays having a common endpoint.	∠CDE	angle CDE

Use the figure to name each.   Answers will vary.
1. 1 ray CD
2. a plane plane ABD
3. 3 points A, C, D
4. 2 lines AB, AC
5. 3 angles ∠ABD, ∠CAB, ∠COB
6. 3 line segments AC, AB, CD

Page 2

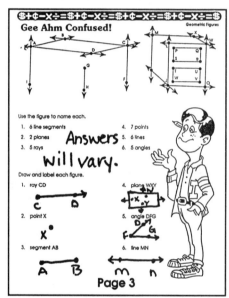

Gee Ahm Confused!

Use the figure to name each.
1. 6 line segments   4. 7 points
2. 2 planes   5. 6 lines
3. 5 rays   6. 5 angles

Answers will vary.

Draw and label each figure.
1. ray CD   4. plane WXY
2. point X   5. angle DFG
3. segment AB   6. line MN

Page 3

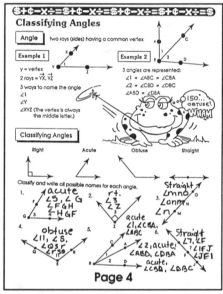

Classifying Angles

Angle — two rays (sides) having a common vertex

Example 1
y = vertex
2 rays = YX, YZ
3 ways to name the angle
∠1
∠Y
∠XYZ (The vertex is always the middle letter.)

Example 2
3 angles are represented:
∠1 = ∠ABC = ∠CBA
∠2 = ∠CBD = ∠DBC
∠ABD = ∠DBA

Classifying Angles

Right   Acute   Obtuse   Straight

Classify and write all possible names for each angle.
1. acute ∠5, ∠G ∠FGH ∠HGF
2. rt. ∠3 ∠Z
   acute ∠1, ∠CBA, ∠ABC
3. Straight ∠mno ∠onm ∠n
4. obtuse ∠11, ∠S, ∠QSr ∠rSQ
5. ∠2, acute; ∠ABD, ∠DBA acute ∠CBD, ∠DBC
6. Straight ∠7, ∠F ∠IFJ ∠JFI

Page 4

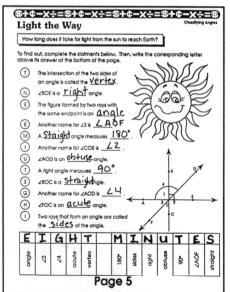

Light the Way

How long does it take for light from the sun to reach Earth?

To find out, complete the statments below. Then, write the corresponding letter above its answer at the bottom of the page.

(T) The intersection of the two sides of an angle is called the **Vertex**.
(N) ∠BOE is a **right** angle.
(E) The figure formed by two rays with the same endpoint is an **angle**.
(E) Another name for ∠3 is **∠AOF**.
(M) A **straight** angle measures **180°**.
(I) Another name for ∠COE is **∠2**.
(U) ∠AOD is an **obtuse** angle.
(T) A right angle measures **90°**.
(S) ∠BOC is a **straight** angle.
(G) Another name for ∠AOD is **∠4**.
(H) ∠FOC is an **acute** angle.
(I) Two rays that form an angle are called the **sides** of the angle.

E	I	G	H	T	M	I	N	U	T	E	S
angle	∠2	∠4	acute	vertex	180°	sides	right	obtuse	90°	∠AOF	straight

Page 5

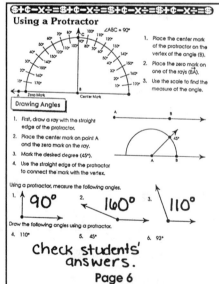

Using a Protractor

∠ABC = 90°

1. Place the center mark of the protractor on the vertex of the angle (B).
2. Place the zero mark on one of the rays (BA).
3. Use the scale to find the measure of the angle.

Zero Mark   Center Mark

Drawing Angles

1. First, draw a ray with the straight edge of the protractor.
2. Place the center mark on point A and the zero mark on the ray.
3. Mark the desired degree (45°).
4. Use the straight edge of the protractor to connect the mark with the vertex.

Using a protractor, measure the following angles.
1. 90°   2. 160°   3. 110°

Draw the following angles using a protractor.
4. 110°   5. 45°   6. 93°

Check students' answers.

Page 6

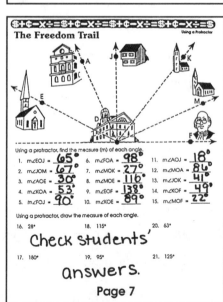

The Freedom Trail

Using a protractor, find the measure (m) of each angle.
1. m∠EOJ = **65**   6. m∠FOA = **98**   11. m∠AOJ = **18**
2. m∠JOM = **67**   7. m∠MOK = **27**   12. m∠MOA = **86**
3. m∠AOE = **30**   8. m∠MOE = **116**   13. m∠JOK = **41**
4. m∠KOA = **53**   9. m∠EOF = **138**   14. m∠KOF = **49**
5. m∠FOJ = **90**   10. m∠KOE = **89**   15. m∠MOF = **22**

Using a protractor, draw the measure of each angle.
16. 28°   18. 115°   20. 63°
17. 180°   19. 95°   21. 125°

Check students' answers.

Page 7

Parallel, Perpendicular and Intersecting Lines

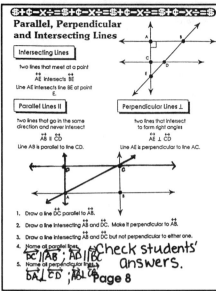

Intersecting Lines

two lines that meet at a point

$\overleftrightarrow{AE}$ intersects $\overleftrightarrow{BE}$

Line AE intersects line BE at point E.

Parallel Lines ∥

two lines that go in the same direction and never intersect

$\overleftrightarrow{AB} \parallel \overleftrightarrow{CD}$

Line AB is parallel to line CD.

Perpendicular Lines ⊥

two lines that intersect to form right angles

$\overleftrightarrow{AE} \perp \overleftrightarrow{CD}$

Line AE is perpendicular to line AC.

1. Draw a line DC parallel to AB.
2. Draw a line intersecting AB and DC. Make it perpendicular to AB.
3. Draw a line intersecting AB and DC but not perpendicular to either one.
4. Name all parallel lines. $\overline{DC} \parallel \overline{AB}$; $\overline{AD} \parallel \overline{BC}$
5. Name all perpendicular lines. $\overline{DA} \perp \overline{CD}$; $\overline{AB} \perp \overline{CD}$

Check students' answers.

Page 8

Following Directions

Parallel, Perpendicular and Intersecting Lines

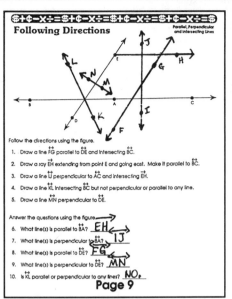

Follow the directions using the figure.

1. Draw a line FG parallel to DE and intersecting BC.
2. Draw a ray EH extending from point E and going east. Make it parallel to BC.
3. Draw a line IJ perpendicular to AC and intersecting EH.
4. Draw a line KL intersecting BC but not perpendicular or parallel to any line.
5. Draw a line MN perpendicular to DE.

Answer the questions using the figure.

6. What line(s) is parallel to BA? EH
7. What line(s) is perpendicular to BA? IJ
8. What line(s) is parallel to DE? FG
9. What line(s) is perpendicular to DE? MN
10. Is KL parallel or perpendicular to any lines? NO.

Page 9

Classifying Triangles

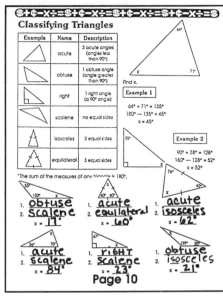

Example	Name	Description
	acute	3 acute angles (angles less than 90°)
	obtuse	1 obtuse angle (angle greater than 90°)
	right	1 right angle (a 90° angle)
	scalene	no equal sides
	isosceles	2 equal sides
	equilateral	3 equal sides

Find x.

Example 1

$64° + 71° = 135°$
$180° - 135° = 45°$
$x = 45°$

Example 2

$90° + 38° = 128°$
$180° - 128° = 52°$
$x = 52°$

*The sum of the measures of any triangle is 180°.

1. obtuse 2. scalene x = 11°
1. acute 2. equilateral x = 60°
1. acute 2. isosceles x = 62°
1. acute 2. scalene x = 84°
1. right 2. scalene x = 23°
1. obtuse 2. isosceles x = 21°

Page 10

Tri These Angles!

Classifying Triangles

Identify each triangle in the puzzle below by writing in the code letters from the box. Identify only the small triangles, not the ones made from smaller ones.

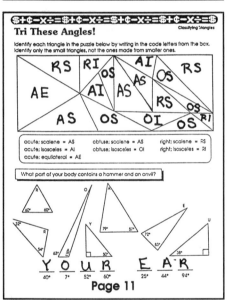

RS	RI		AI		RS
OS				OS	
AE	AI	AS	AS		
				RS	OS
AS	OS	OI	OS	RI	

acute; scalene = AS
acute; isosceles = AI
acute; equilateral = AE
obtuse; scalene = AS
obtuse; isosceles = OI
right; scalene = RS
right; isosceles = RI

What part of your body contains a hammer and an anvil?

Y O U R   E A R
40° 7° 52° 8°   25° 44° 94°

Page 11

Classifying Quadrilaterals

Classifying Quadrilaterals

Name	Description	Example
trapezoid	1 pair of opposite sides parallel	
parallelogram	• opposite sides parallel • opposite sides and opposite angles congruent	
rhombus	parallelogram with all sides congruent	
rectangle	parallelogram with four right angles	
square	rectangle with four congruent sides	

*The sum of the measures of the angles in any quadrilateral is 360°.

Find x.

Example 1

$93° + 39° + 160° = 292°$
$360° - 292° = 68°$
$x = 68°$

Example 2

$90° + 90° + 56° = 236°$
$360° - 236° = 124°$
$x = 124°$

Give all the names for each quadrilateral. Then, find each missing angle measure.

1. 103° trapezoid
2. 128° parallel.
3. 90° square, rect., rhomb., parallel.
4. 90° rect.; parallel.
5. 54° trap.
6. 119° trapezoid

Page 12

Woodpeckers Delight

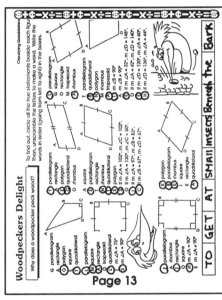

Why does a woodpecker peck wood?

TO GET AT SMALL INSECTS BENEATH THE BARK

Page 13

Polyhedrons

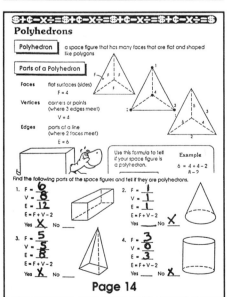

Polyhedron — a space figure that has many faces that are flat and shaped like polygons

Parts of a Polyhedron

Faces — flat surfaces (sides) F = 4

Vertices — corners or points (where 3 edges meet) V = 4

Edges — parts of a line (where 2 faces meet) E = 6

Use this formula to tell if a space figure is a polyhedron.

Example

$6 = 4 + 4 - 2$
$8 = 2$

Find the following parts of the space figures and tell if they are polyhedrons.

1. F = 6 V = 8 E = 12 E = F + V − 2 Yes X No ___
2. F = 1 V = 1 E = 1 E = F + V − 2 Yes ___ No X
3. F = 5 V = 5 E = 8 E = F + V − 2 Yes X No ___
4. F = 3 V = 0 E = 2 E = F + V − 2 Yes ___ No X

Page 14

What a Bill!

Polyhedrons

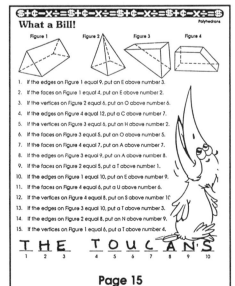

Figure 1   Figure 2   Figure 3   Figure 4

1. If the edges on Figure 1 equal 9, put an E above number 3.
2. If the faces on Figure 1 equal 4, put an E above number 2.
3. If the vertices on Figure 2 equal 6, put an O above number 6.
4. If the edges on Figure 4 equal 12, put a C above number 7.
5. If the vertices on Figure 3 equal 6, put an H above number 2.
6. If the faces on Figure 3 equal 5, put an O above number 4.
7. If the faces on Figure 4 equal 7, put an A above number 7.
8. If the edges on Figure 3 equal 9, put an A above number 8.
9. If the vertices on Figure 2 equal 5, put a T above number 1.
10. If the edges on Figure 1 equal 10, put an E above number 4.
11. If the faces on Figure 4 equal 6, put a U above number 6.
12. If the vertices on Figure 4 equal 8, put an S above number 10.
13. If the edges on Figure 3 equal 10, put a T above number 3.
14. If the faces on Figure 2 equal 4, put an N above number 9.
15. If the vertices on Figure 1 equal 6, put a T above number 4.

T H E   T O U C A N S
1 2 3   4 5 6 7 8 9 10

Page 15

Graphing Ordered Pairs

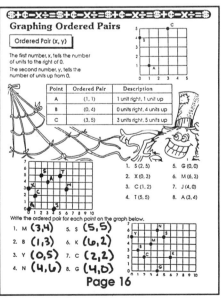

Ordered Pair (x, y)

The first number, x, tells the number of units to the right of 0.

The second number, y, tells the number of units up from 0.

Point	Ordered Pair	Description
A	(1, 1)	1 unit right, 1 unit up
B	(0, 4)	0 units right, 4 units up
C	(3, 5)	3 units right, 5 units up

1. S (2, 5)   5. P (5, 0)
2. X (0, 3)   6. M (6, 3)
3. C (1, 2)   7. J (4, 0)
4. T (5, 5)   8. A (3, 4)

Write the ordered pair for each point on the graph below.

1. M (3, 4)   5. S (5, 5)
2. B (1, 3)   6. K (6, 2)
3. Y (0, 5)   7. C (2, 2)
4. N (4, 6)   8. G (4, 0)

Page 16

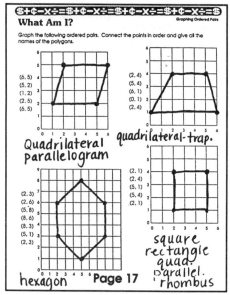

What Am I?
Graphing Ordered Pairs

Graph the following ordered pairs. Connect the points in order and give all the names of the polygons.

(6, 5) (5, 2) (1, 2) (2, 5) (6, 5)

Quadrilateral parallelogram

(2, 4) (5, 4) (6, 1) (0, 1) (2, 4)

quadrilateral-trap.

(2, 3) (2, 6) (5, 8) (8, 6) (8, 3) (5, 1) (2, 3)

hexagon

(2, 1) (2, 4) (5, 1) (5, 4) (2, 1)

square rectangle quad parallel. rhombus

Page 17

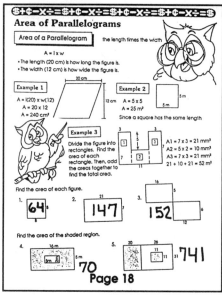

Area of Parallelograms

Area of a Parallelogram — the length times the width

A = l x w

- The length (20 cm) is how long the figure is.
- The width (12 cm) is how wide the figure is.

Example 1
A = l(20) x w(12)
A = 20 x 12
A = 240 cm²

Example 2
A = 5 x 5
A = 25 m²
Since a square has the same length

Example 3
Divide the figure into rectangles. Find the area of each rectangle. Then, add the areas together to find the total area.
A1 = 7 x 3 = 21 m³
A2 = 5 x 2 = 10 m³
A3 = 7 x 3 = 21 m³
21 + 10 + 21 = 52 m³

Find the area of each figure.
1. **64** 2. **147** 3. **152**

Find the area of the shaded region.
4. **70** 5. **741**

Page 18

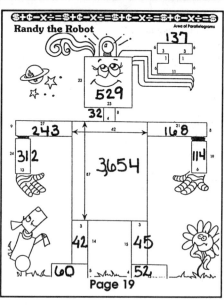

Randy the Robot
Area of Parallelograms

137
529
32
243 168
312 3654 114
42 45
60 52

Page 19

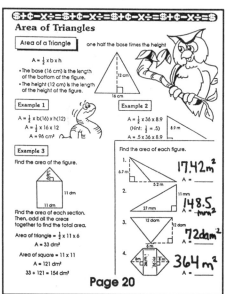

Area of Triangles

Area of a Triangle — one half the base times the height

A = ½ x b x h

- The base (16 cm) is the length of the bottom of the figure.
- The height (12 cm) is the length of the height of the figure.

Example 1
A = ½ x b(16) x h(12)
A = ½ 16 x 12
A = 96 cm²

Example 2
A = ½ x 36 x 8.9
(Hint: ½ = .5)
A = .5 x 36 x 8.9
A = 154 m²

Example 3
Find the area of the figure.

Find the area of each section. Then, add all the areas together to find the total area.

Area of triangle = ½ x 11 x 6
A = 33 dm²

Area of square = 11 x 11
A = 121 dm²
33 + 121 = 154 dm²

Find the area of each figure.
1. **17.42 m²**
2. **148.5 m²**
3. **72 dam²**
4. **364 m²**

Page 20

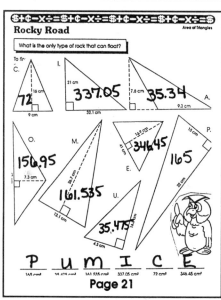

Rocky Road
Area of Triangles

What is the only type of rock that can float?

C. **72** I. **337.05** A. **35.34**
O. **156.95** M. **161.535** **346.45** P. **165** E. U. **35.475**

P U M I C E
165 cm² 35.475 cm² 161.535 cm² 337.05 cm² 72 cm² 346.45 cm²

Page 21

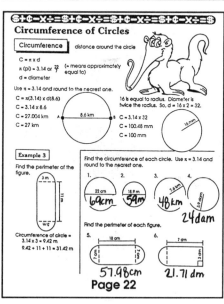

Circumference of Circles

Circumference — distance around the circle

C = π x d
π (pi) ≈ 3.14 or 22/7 (≈ means approximately equal to)
d = diameter

Use π = 3.14 and round to the nearest one.
C = π(3.14) x d(8.6)
C = 3.14 x 8.6
C = 27.004 km
C ≈ 27 km

16 is equal to radius. Diameter is twice the radius. So, d = 16 x 2 = 32.
C = 3.14 x 32
C = 100.48 mm
C ≈ 100 mm

Example 3
Find the perimeter of the figure.
Circumference of circle = 3.14 x 9.42 m
9.42 + 11 + 11 = 31.42 m

Find the circumference of each circle. Use π = 3.14 and round to the nearest one.
1. **69 cm** 2. **59 m** 3. **48 km** 4. **24 dam**

Find the perimeter of each figure.
5. **57.98 cm** 6. **21.71 dm**

Page 22

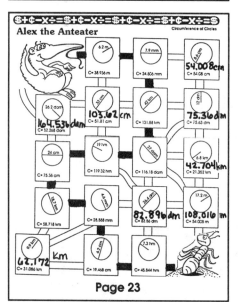

Alex the Anteater
Circumference of Circles

6.2 m C = 38.936 m
7.9 m C = 24.806 mm
54.008 cm C = 54.08 cm
26.2 dam **103.62 cm** C = 51.81 cm C = 131.88 km **75.36 dm** C = 75.63 mm
164.536 dam C = 52.268 dam
24 19 **42.704 km**
C = 75.36 m C = 119.32 hm C = 116.18 km 6.8 km C = 21.352 km
82.896 dm **108.016 m**
C = 58.718 km C = 28.588 mm C = 52.56 dm 17.2 m C = 54.008 m
62.172 **Km**
C = 31.066 km C = 19.468 mm C = 45.844 hm

Page 23

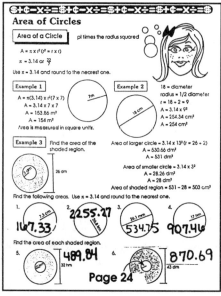

Area of Circles

Area of a Circle — pi times the radius squared

A = π x r² (r² = r x r)
π ≈ 3.14 or 22/7
Use π = 3.14 and round to the nearest one.

Example 1
A = π(3.14) x r²(7 x 7)
A = 3.14 x 7 x 7
A = 153.86 m²

Example 2
18 = diameter
radius = ½ diameter
r = 18 ÷ 2 = 9
A = 3.14 x 9²
A = 254.34 cm²
A ≈ 254 cm²
Area is measured in square units.

Example 3 Find the area of the shaded region.
Area of larger circle = 3.14 x 13² (r = 26 ÷ 2)
A = 530.66 m²
Area of smaller circle = 3.14 x 3²
A = 28.26 m²
A = 28 dm²
Area of shaded region = 531 – 28 = 503 cm²

Find the following areas. Use π = 3.14 and round to the nearest one.
1. **167.33** 2. **2255.27** 3. **534.75** 4. **907.46**

Find the area of each shaded region.
5. **489.84** 6. **870.69**

Page 24

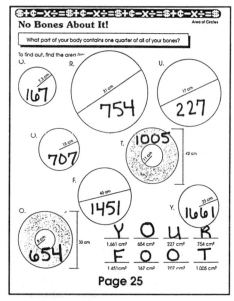

No Bones About It!
Area of Circles

What part of your body contains one quarter of all of your bones?

To find out, find the area.

O. **167** R. **754** U. **227**
O. **707** T. **1005**
F. **1451** Y. **1661**
O. **654**

Y O U R
1,661 cm² 654 cm² 227 cm² 754 cm²

F O O T
1,451 cm² 167 cm² 707 cm² 1,005 cm²

Page 25

Page 26 — Relating Customary Units of Length

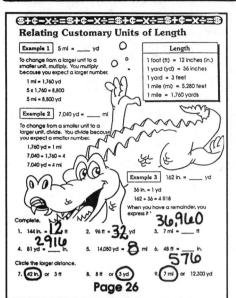

Example 1 5 mi = ___ yd

To change from a larger unit to a smaller unit, multiply. You multiply because you expect a larger number.

1 mi = 1,760 yd
5 × 1,760 = 8,800
5 mi = 8,800 yd

Example 2 7,040 yd = ___ mi

To change from a smaller unit to a larger unit, divide. You divide because you expect a smaller number.

1,760 yd = 1 mi
7,040 ÷ 1,760 = 4
7,040 yd = 4 mi

Length
1 foot (ft) = 12 inches (in.)
1 yard (yd) = 36 inches
1 yard = 3 feet
1 mile (mi) = 5,280 feet
1 mile = 1,760 yards

Example 3 162 in. = ___ yd

36 in. = 1 yd
162 ÷ 36 = 4 R18
When you have a remainder, you express it 4 36/960

Complete.
1. 144 in. = **12** ft
2. 96 ft = **32** yd
3. 7 mi = **36,960** in.
4. 81 yd = **2,916** in.
5. 14,080 ft = **8** mi
6. 48 ft = **576** in.

Circle the larger distance.
7. **(42 in.)** or 3 ft
8. 8 ft or **(3 yd)**
9. **(7 mi)** or 12,300 yd

Page 27 — Puzzling Lengths

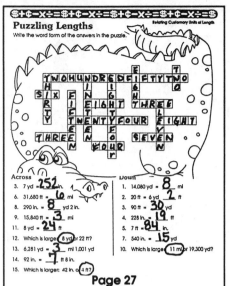

Relating Customary Units of Length

Write the word form of the answers in the puzzle.

Crossword answers: TWOHUNDREDFIFTYTWO, SIX, FIFTEEN, EIGHT, THREE, THIRTY, TWENTYFOUR, EIGHT, THREE, SEVEN, FOUR

Across
5. 7 yd = **252**
6. 31,680 ft = **6** mi
8. 290 in. = **8** yd 2 in.
9. 15,840 ft = **3** mi
11. 8 yd = **24**
12. Which is larger: **8 yd** or 22 ft?
13. 6,281 in. = **3** mi 1,001 in.
14. 92 in. = **7** ft 8 in.
15. Which is larger: 42 in. or **4 ft**?

Down
1. 14,080 ft = **8** mi
2. 20 ft = 6 yd **2** ft
3. 90 ft = **30** yd
4. 228 in. = **19** ft
5. 7 ft = **84** in.
7. 540 in. = **15** yd
10. Which is larger: **11 mi** or 19,300 ft?

Page 28 — Relating Customary Units of Weight and Capacity

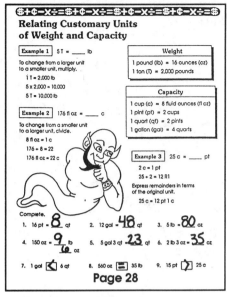

Example 1 5 T = ___ lb

To change from a larger unit to a smaller unit, multiply.

1 T = 2,000 lb
5 × 2,000 = 10,000
5 T = 10,000 lb

Example 2 176 fl oz = ___ c

To change from a smaller unit to a larger unit, divide.

8 fl oz = 1 c
176 ÷ 8 = 22
176 fl oz = 22 c

Weight
1 pound (lb) = 16 ounces (oz)
1 ton (T) = 2,000 pounds

Capacity
1 cup (c) = 8 fluid ounces (fl oz)
1 pint (pt) = 2 cups
1 quart (qt) = 2 pints
1 gallon (gal) = 4 quarts

Example 3 25 c = ___ pt

2 c = 1 pt
25 ÷ 2 = 12 R1
Express remainders in terms of the original unit.
25 c = 12 pt 1 c

Complete.
1. 16 pt = **8** qt
2. 12 gal = **48** qt
3. 5 lb = **80** oz
4. 150 oz = **9 6/16** lb
5. 5 gal 3 qt = **23** qt
6. 2 lb 3 oz = **35** oz
7. 1 gal **(=)** 6 qt
8. 560 oz **( )** 35 lb
9. 15 pt **(>)** 25 c

Page 29

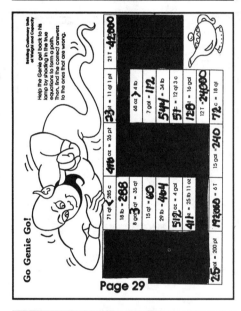

Relating Customary Units of Weight and Capacity

Help the Genie get back to his lamp by shading in the true equations to form a path. Then, find the correct answers to the ones that are wrong.

Go Genie Go!

21 T = **42,000**
11 qt = 11 qt 1 pt
68 oz = **4** lb
7 gal = **172**
5 gal = **544** = 34 qt
5 T = **128** = 12 qt 3 c
12 T = **24,000**
15 gal = **240** = 18 qt
12 T = **72**
285 c = **288**
8 lb = **128**
15 qt = **60**
29 lb = **464**
5 gal = **512** = 4 gal
41 lb = **25** lb 11 oz
71 qt = 26 pt
18 lb = 19 qt
23 qt = 11 gal 1 pt
47 lb = 40 oz
26 gal = 200 pt
26 gal = **6 T**

Page 30 — Relating Metric Units of Length

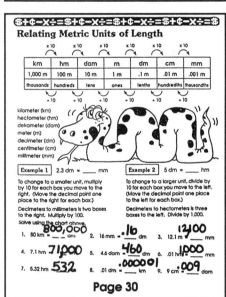

	km	hm	dam	m	dm	cm	mm
	1,000 m	100 m	10 m	1 m	.1 m	.01 m	.001 m
	thousands	hundreds	tens	ones	tenths	hundredths	thousandths

kilometer (km)
hectometer (hm)
dekameter (dam)
meter (m)
decimeter (dm)
centimeter (cm)
millimeter (mm)

Example 1 2.3 dm = ___ mm

To change to a smaller unit, multiply by 10 for each box you move to the right. (Move the decimal point one place to the right for each box.)
Decimeters to millimeters is two boxes to the right. Multiply by 100.

Example 2 5 dm = ___ hm

To change to a larger unit, divide by 10 for each box you move to the left. (Move the decimal point one place to the left for each box.)
Decimeters to hectometers is three boxes to the left. Divide by 1,000.

Solve using the chart above.
1. 80 km = **800,000**
2. 16 mm = **.16** dm
3. 12.1 m = **12,100** mm
4. 7.1 hm = **71,000**
5. 4.6 dam = **460** dm
6. .01 km = **1,000**
7. 5.32 km = **532**
8. .01 cm = **.000001**
9. 9 cm = **.009** dam

Page 31 — Bulls-Eye

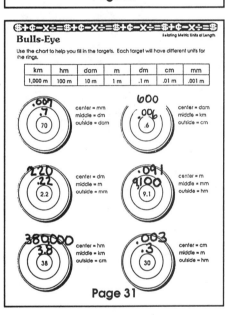

Relating Metric Units of Length

Use the chart to help you fill in the targets. Each target will have different units for the rings.

km	hm	dam	m	dm	cm	mm
1,000 m	100 m	10 m	1 m	.1 m	.01 m	.001 m

Target 1: .007 / .7 / 70 — center = mm, middle = dm, outside = dam
Target 2: 600 / .006 / .6 — center = dam, middle = km, outside = cm
Target 3: 2,200 / 22 / 2.2 — center = dm, middle = m, outside = m
Target 4: .091 / 9,100 / 9.1 — center = m, middle = cm, outside = hm
Target 5: 380,000 / 3.8 / 38 — center = hm, middle = cm, outside = cm
Target 6: .003 / .3 / 30 — center = cm, middle = m, outside = hm

Page 32 — Relating Metric Units of Mass (Weight) and Capacity

kg	hg	dag	g	dg	cg	mg
kL	hL	daL	L	dL	cL	mL
1,000	100	10	1	.1	.01	.001
thousands	hundreds	tens	ones	tenths	hundredths	thousandths

kilogram (kg)   decigram (dg)   kiloliter (kL)   deciliter (dL)
hectogram (hg)   centigram (cg)   hectoliter (hL)   centiliter (cL)

Example 1 .06 dag = ___ cg

To change to a smaller unit, multiply by 10 for each box you move to the right. (Move the decimal point one place to the right for each box.)
Dekagrams to centigrams is three boxes to the right. Multiply by 1,000.
.06 × 1,000 = 60
.06 dag = 60 cg

Example 2 81 dL = ___ kL

To change to a larger unit, divide by 10 for each box you move to the left. (Move the decimal point one place to the left for each box.)
Deciliters to kiloliters is four boxes to the left. Divide by 10,000.
81 ÷ 10,000 = .0081
81 dL = .0081 kL

Solve using the chart above.
1. 16 dg = **1,600** mg
2. 6.1 mL = **.000061** hL
3. 16.8 hL = **168,000** cL
4. 8.9 dag = **890**
5. 16 kg = **14,000**
6. 9 L = **.09** hL
7. .8 cL = **.0008**
8. 9 g = **9,000**
9. .06 hg = **6,000** mg

Page 33 — An Amazing Animal

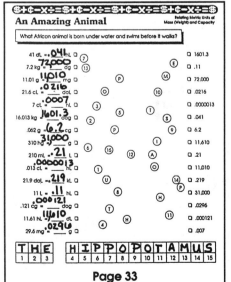

Relating Metric Units of Mass (Weight) and Capacity

What African animal is born under water and swims before it walks?

41 dL = **.041** hL
7.2 kg = **72,000**
11.01 cL = **11,010** mg
21.6 cL = **.0216**
16.013 kg = **1,601.3**
.062 g = **6.2** cg
310 mL = **31,000**
210 mL = **.21** L
.013 cL = **.000013**
21.9 daL = **219** kL
11 L = **.11** hL
.121 cg = **.000121** dag
11.61 hL = **11,610**
29.6 mg = **.0296** g

Answer boxes: 1601.3, .11, 72,000, .0216, .0000013, .041, 6.2, 11,610, .21, 11,010, .219, 31,000, .0296, .000121, .007

THE HIPPOPOTAMUS

Page 34 — Ratios

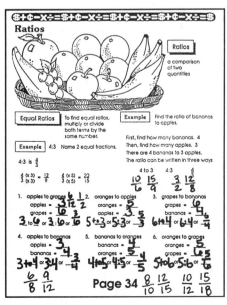

a comparison of two quantities

Equal Ratios To find equal ratios, multiply or divide both terms by the same number.

Example 4:3 Name 2 equal fractions.

4:3 is 4/3

4/3 (×3) = 12/9   4/3 (×5) = 20/15

Example Find the ratio of bananas to apples.

First, find how many bananas. 4
Then, find how many apples. 3
There are 4 bananas to 3 apples.
The ratio can be written in three ways.

4 to 3   4:3   4/3

10/6   15/9   3/2   1 1/2

1. apples to grapes 6/6 = 1/1
2. oranges to apples 5/5
3. grapes to bananas 6/4
   3 to 6 or 3:6 to 1/6   5÷3 or 5:3 or 5/3   6÷4 or 6:4 or 6/4
4. apples to bananas 3/4
5. bananas to oranges 4/5
6. oranges to grapes 5/6
   3÷4 or 3:4 or 3/4   4÷5 or 4:5 or 4/5   5÷6 or 5:6 or 5/6
   6/8 9/12   8/10 12/15   10/12 15/18

Page 35 — Hhmm?

Ratios

What do the four H's stand for in the 4-H Club?

E. tennis shoes to sandals 3:6
N. bare feet to men's dress shoes 5:1
S. high heels to tennis shoes 2:3
E. sandals to bare feet 6:5
E. men's dress shoes to high heels 1:2
A. high heels to sandals 2:6
T. bare feet to tennis shoes 5:3
A. high heels to bare feet 2:5
D. tennis shoes to men's dress shoes 3:1
H. men's dress shoes to sandals 1:6
H. bare feet to sandals 5:6
R. sandals to high heels 6:2
H. tennis shoes to high heels 3:2
D. sandals to tennis shoes 6:3
T. men's dress shoes to tennis shoes 1:3
H. tennis shoes to bare feet 3:5
L. high heels to men's dress shoes 2:1
A. men's dress shoes to bare feet 1:5
A. bare feet to high heels 5:2
H. sandals to men's dress shoes 6:1

H E A D,   H E A R T,
3:5 6:5 2:3 5:1   3:1 1:6 5:6 6:2 5:3

H E A L T H,   H A N D S
3:2 6:3 2:5 2:1 1:3 6:1   3:2 2:5 5:2 6:3 2:3

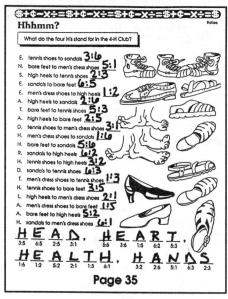

Page 36 — Proportion

Proportion states that two ratios are equal.

Example 1   Is $\frac{8}{10} = \frac{4}{5}$ a proportion?

To test for a proportion, use equal ratios or cross products. In a proportion, cross products are equal.

Equal Ratios

$\frac{8}{10} = \frac{4}{5}$

$\frac{8}{10} (\div 2) = \frac{4}{5}$

Cross Products

$\frac{8}{10} \times \frac{4}{5}$

$8 \times 5 = 10 \times 4$
$40 = 40$

The ratios are equal.

Example 2   Is $\frac{2}{3} = \frac{10}{16}$ a proportion?

$2 \times 16 \quad \boxed{\quad} \quad 3 \times 10$
$32 \neq 30$
No.

Compare. Fill in each box with = or ≠ to make a true statement.

1. $\frac{5}{8} \boxed{=} \frac{15}{24}$
2. $\frac{8}{9} \boxed{=} \frac{24}{27}$
3. $\frac{6}{7} \boxed{\neq} \frac{13}{14}$

4. $\frac{12}{14} \boxed{=} \frac{18}{21}$
5. $\frac{9}{32} \boxed{\neq} \frac{12}{64}$
6. $\frac{5}{15} \boxed{=} \frac{7}{35}$

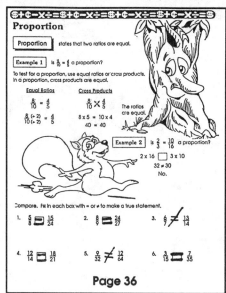

Page 37 — Sam the Squirrel

Proportion

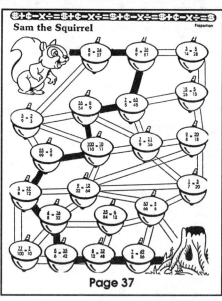

Page 38 — Map Scales

Map Scales are used to estimate distances on a map.

It compares the distance on a map with the actual distance.

This map has a scale of 1 to 4, or 1:4 or $\frac{1}{4}$.

—⊢ 1 cm = 4 miles

Example   How many miles long is Road A?

1. Use a ruler to measure the distance on the map.
   9 cm
2. Write a proportion using the scale as a ratio.
   $\frac{\text{scale}}{\text{actual}} \quad \frac{1}{4} = \frac{9}{x}$
3. Solve the proportion.
   $\frac{1}{4} = \frac{9}{x}$
   $1 \times x = 4 \times 9$
   $x = 36$
   Road A is 36 miles long.

Use the map above to answer the following questions.

1. How many miles long is Road B?   26
2. How many miles long is Road C?   17
3. How many miles long is Road D?   21
4. How many miles long are   52

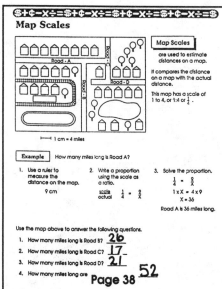

Page 39 — Map It Out!

Map Scales

Make your own map using the map scale that is given.

—⊢ 1 cm = 2.5 miles

1. Draw a road 16 miles long going east to west between the park and the neighborhood. Label it Hill Road.
2. Draw a road 21 miles long going north to south starting from the schoolhouse. Label it Schoolhouse Drive.
3. Draw a road 18 miles long perpendicular to and intersecting Hill Road. Make sure it starts from the houses. Label it Neighborhood Road.
4. Draw a public swimming pool 10 miles northeast of the park.
5. Draw a playground 12 miles south of the swimming pool and 8 miles south of the park.
6. Draw a soccer field :   od.
7. Draw a fountain 11 r   17.5 miles from the schoolhouse.

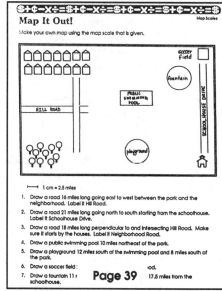

Page 40 — Mean, Median, Mode and Range

Example   Jim had the following test scores in math: 100, 90, 68, 70, 80, 84, 100, 100, 100. Find the mean, median, mode and range of his scores.

Mean   same as average

First, add up all the scores.
$100 + 90 + 68 + 70 + 80 + 84 + 100 + 100 + 100 = 792$
Then, divide by the number of tests.
$792 \div 9 = 88$

Median   the middle score

First, arrange scores in order.
68, 70, 80, 84, 90, 100, 100, 100, 100
Then, find the middle number. 90

(Hint: If there is not one middle number, add the two middle numbers and divide by two. Example: 2, 4, 5, 9)
$4 + 5 = 9 \div 2 = 4.5$ 4.5 is median.

Mode   the score that occurs most often
100

Range   the difference between the highest and the lowest score
$100 − 68 = 32$

1. 3, 4, 7, 3, 3, 4, 2, 3
   mean 3.625
   median 3
   mode 3
   range 5

2. 45, 45, 22, 18, 46, 31
   mean 34.5
   median 38
   mode 45
   range 28

3. 28, 26, 30, 28, 27, 29, 28
   mean 28
   median 28
   mode 28
   range 4

4. 150, 200, 150, 150, 210, 304, 173
   mean 191
   median 173
   mode 150
   range 154

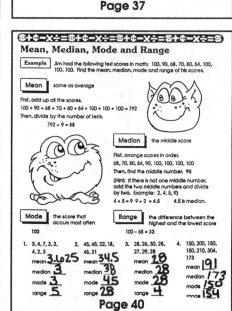

Page 41 — Mean, Median, Mode and Range

Find the mean, median, mode and range of the numbers in the stars that are attached by stardust and put the answers in the shapes.

Solar RM³

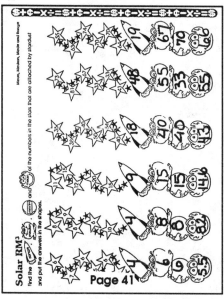

70
69
76

48
55
33
85

40
49
90

15
18
44

60
82

95
55

Page 42 — Broken-Line, Bar and Circle Graphs

BAR GRAPH

RAINFALL IN INCHES

MONTHS

BROKEN-LINE GRAPH

RAINFALL IN INCHES

MONTHS

Favorite Time For Study

15% before school
35% after dinner
25% after school
15% during school
10% other

Circle Graph

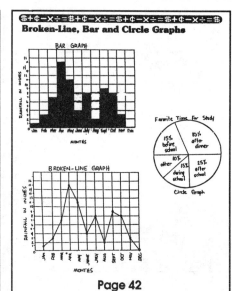

Page 43 — Graphs Galore!

Broken-Line, Bar and Circle Graphs

Make each of the following graphs using the information given. Then, answer the questions using the graphs.

Broken-Line Graph
TEMPERATURES IN ST. LOUIS FOR ONE WEEK

Saturday	63°
Sunday	65°
Monday	61°
Tuesday	63°
Wednesday	70°
Thursday	68°
Friday	65°

Bar Graph
TOTAL NUMBER OF HITS FOR ONE SEASON

Sally	18
Sue	16
Jill	23
Mary	15
Lee	31
Janie	23
Judy	33

Circle Graph
SIXTH GRADERS' FAVORITE CLASS IN SCHOOL

Math	20%
History	10%
Science	30%
Reading	20%
Physical Ed.	10%
Music	5%
Art	5%

1. Who had the most number of hits in one season?   Judy
2. What day was the warmest?   WEDNESDAY
3. What percent of sixth graders like math and music?   25%
4. What day was the coldest?   MONDAY
5. What percent of sixth graders like science and art?   35%
6. What two players had the same number of hits?   Jill + JANIE
7. What is the difference between the highest and lowest temperatures?   9°
8. What is the sixth graders' favorite class?   SCIENCE
9. Who had the least number of hits in one season?   MARY
10. On what two days was the temperature 63°?   SAT. + TUE.

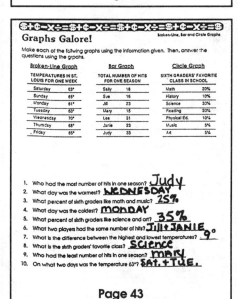